Open a Can of Worms

by Debbie Caffrey

Debbie's Creative Moments, Inc.
P.O. Box 92050
Albuquerque, NM 87199-2050

www.debbiescreativemoments.com

Acknowledgements

Thank you to those who helped me meet my deadlines by quilting some of the quilts. Norma Kindred of Eagle River, Alaska, quilted *Stacked Coins*, *Friendship Braid*, and *Cobblestones*; Mary Johnson of Sutton, Alaska, quilted *Square Knots*, *Trees*, and *Sister's Choice*; and Karen Tomczak of Anchorage, Alaska, quilted *Four on Point*, *Four Patches & Friends*, and *Road to Oklahoma*.

Thank you, too, to Dottie Tessandore of Anchorage, Alaska, who pieced her version of *Four Patches & Friends* in one of my mystery classes and has graciously allowed me to show it.

Dedication

To my dear friend Sally Klinger of Anchorage, Alaska, who has championed my teaching and publishing efforts since I first began. More than that, she has always been a friend first.

Open a Can of Worms

©2000 by Debbie Caffrey

Credits

Photographed by

Ken Wagner Photography
Seattle, Washington

Ken photographed all the quilts except Dottie Tessandore's
Four Patches & Friends.

Chris Arend Photography
Anchorage, Alaska

Chris photographed
Dottie Tessandore's
Four Patches & Friends.

Gayle Stubbs
Anchorage, Alaska
Gayle did the black and white photography.

Printed by

Palmer Printing
St. Cloud, Minnesota

Illustrated by

Debbie Caffrey

Proofread by

Erin Caffrey

Published by

Debbie's Creative Moments, Inc.
P.O. Box 92050
Albuquerque, NM 87199-2050
USA

ISBN: 0-9645777-4-7

First Printing, 2000

Table of Contents

What is a Worm?   4

General Instructions   6

Color Photo Gallery   17

Quilt Patterns   29

    Stacked Coins   29
    Cobblestones   32
    Square Knots   36
    Four Patches & Friends   40
    Buzz Saw   45
    Friendship Braid   49
    Sister's Choice   53
    Road to Oklahoma   57
    Trees   61
    Four on Point   66
    Star Sampler   70

Templates   75

What is a Worm?

And, what does it have to do with quilting?

A *worm* is a strip of fabric that is two and a half inches wide. How did I happen to come to that definition? Well, once I began to slice and dice these strips, the quilts just wouldn't stop coming. I felt that I had truly "opened a can of worms". Not only did I make the quilts that are in this book, but I have enough other patterns to be halfway through a sequel.

It doesn't stop there. I have a couple dozen quilts that are made from two inch wide strips, too. By the way, in case anyone asks, two inch wide strips are "noodles". That definition came about while designing and constructing a mystery quilt pattern. The many strips on my cutting table reminded me of Grandma's homemade noodles drying on the kitchen table. So I named the mystery *Noodle Soup*. But, "noodles" are for another day and another book -- back to the worms.

There were many thoughts that led to this book. First of all, there's the popularity of fabric exchanges. I have read in many magazines about the desire to exchange squares. I guess I'm just too impatient to work with such small pieces, but I refuse keep track of them. They go into a box and are sent off to a friend who does foundation paper piecing. Instead, I would prefer to gather with friends and cut strips from a yard of several different fabrics and exchange those. This is a great activity for quilt groups and guilds. I have been told that there are some rowdy quilters out there who play their version of strip poker using fabric strips in place of chips or money. If poker isn't your game try bingo, trivia games, or some other competition.

Secondly, friendship quilts are quite popular. The quilts in this book are very conducive to making group quilts. With the donation of a fcw strips from everyone involved, the quilt is finished quickly, and it represents a part of each participant.

Next, I was asked by quilters in my workshops how I dealt with small lengths of fabric in my stash. I realized that rarely do I find the small pieces that are sandwiched in between larger pieces of yardage. What do they get used for anyway? Scrap quilts! By cutting the leftovers into strips they are in an organized and ready state for a project.

Then came a great revelation. I became aware of triangle tools that would allow me to cut triangles and trapezoids from strips of fabric. This added a whole new dimension to the shapes I could extract from my strips.

It goes without saying that I am really excited about this concept. Not only does it get you organized, but your quilts become more interesting. Consider this: A pattern asks for a dozen strips (worms) of green. The easy way is to use a yard of one fabric and cut the strips. But, fabric lover that I am, I would really rather have one strip each of twelve different fabrics. Now I just get my box of green worms and pull out a dozen strips. What could be easier?

Oh, and remember those fabulous fabrics that you had to have? You know, the ones that when you looked at them a few months later you wondered whatever possessed you to buy them in the first place? Cut them up and you'll remember why. Some of the fabrics I began to cut from my stash had copyright dates from the eighties. What am I saving them for?

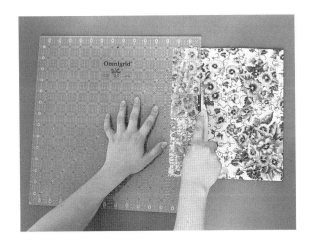

Please take the time to read the general instructions prior to making any of these quilts. The chapter is packed with techniques and tips that are absolutely essential to these patterns and will really speed up your construction while improving your precision.

You probably can't imagine that there is much more to be said about strip cutting, but those in my workshops say that the strip cutting information alone is "worth the price of admission".

Important Cutting Information!!!

The cutting information in this book is very different from most patterns. Please acquaint yourself with the concepts, techniques, and terms. Study what is below and be sure to read pages 10 through 13 before cutting and piecing any of the quilts in this book!

Squares and rectangles -- The cutting information in the patterns is exactly as you would expect. Almost everything is cut from 2 1/2" wide strips. The sizes for squares and rectangles given in the cutting instructions are the exact sizes that you should cut the pieces. They will finish 1/2" smaller than the cut size because of 1/4" seam allowances on all sides. Example: The instructions tell you to cut a rectangle 2 1/2" x 4 1/2". When the quilt is finished, the rectangle will measure 2" x 4". There's nothing different about this.

Half-square triangles -- I use a specialty tool to cut these pieces, therefore, they are cut differently than you would with normal rotary cutting instructions. My instructions will tell you to cut a **2" (finished size) half-square triangle. That is the finished size of the two short sides of the piece.** You are probably familiar with cutting a 2 7/8" square once, diagonally, to achieve these pieces. Because of the limitation of working from 2 1/2" strips the pieces must be cut with a triangle tool or template 2 on page 75. The Omnigrid 96 that I use is marked by the finished size and has the seam allowances built into those markings. Study the information on page 10 until you are sure that you understand the cutting method. When all else fails, compare the fabric piece that you cut with the triangle tool to template 2 to be reassured that it is the correct size.

Trapezoids -- These shapes are also cut with a triangle tool or template. My instructions will tell you to cut a **4" (finished size) trapezoid or 6" (finished size) trapezoid. That is the finished size of the longest side of the piece.** If you measure the longest side of this piece you will find that the cut sizes actually measure 4 7/8" and 6 7/8", respectively, to allow for seam allowances. Study the information on page 11 until you are sure that you understand the cutting method. Compare the fabric piece that you cut with the triangle tool to its respective template to be reassured that it is the correct size.

Quarter-square triangles -- These pieces are cut using a second triangle tool, the Omnigrid 98, or a template. My instructions will tell you to cut a **4" (finished size) quarter-square triangle. That is the finished size of the long side of the piece.** You are probably familiar with cutting a 5 1/4" square twice, diagonally, to achieve these pieces. Again, because of working from 2 1/2" strips the pieces must be cut with a triangle tool or template A on page 75. The Omnigrid 98 is marked with the finished size and has the seam allowances built into those markings. Study the information on page 12 until you are sure that you understand the cutting method. Compare the fabric piece that you cut with the triangle tool to template A to be reassured that it is the correct size.

General Instructions

It is very important to take the time to review the general instructions prior to using the patterns. Many of the questions that can arise by going directly to the construction of the quilts will be answered in this chapter.

Fabric Yardage & Preparation

Except for the worms, which obviously have no excess yardage allowance, fabric yardage is fairly generous allowing for shrinkage, straightening, and minor goofs.

I prefer to wash and press my fabrics prior to using them. It is a habit I began when I first started quilting, and if for no other reason, I continue to wash them because I don't care to use washed and unwashed fabrics together in the same project. I have made quilts using only new, unwashed fabric, and I have to say I did not like handling the fabrics.

To avoid distorting your fabric as you press the yardage, move your iron in strokes that are parallel to the selvages. This is in the direction of the stable warp yarns that do not stretch with the iron's strokes. Too often I have had quilters come to class with fabrics that seem to have wavy, wobbly edges along the selvages. Most of the time this problem is not due to the quality of the fabric. It is created by moving the iron from side to side between the selvages while applying any combination of the following: heavy pressure, steam, and starch or sizing.

Steam, starch, and sizing are fine, but take care that you do not distort the fabric. Some of the patterns will require you to sew along the bias edges of triangles and trapezoids. Spray starching your fabrics prior to cutting them will help stabilize them against stretching as you sew.

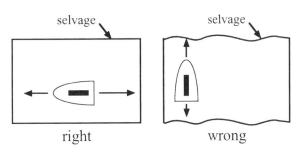

right   wrong

Cutting

The quilts in this book are all designed for rotary cutting and machine piecing. Most of you are quite familiar with your rotary cutter. With that in mind, you may be surprised that I have elected to talk about strip cutting. This is the "worth the price of admission" information that I spoke about in the introduction.

When cutting strips for a project, I use my 15" square ruler. The same technique can be used with most square rulers that are 12" or larger.

Begin by folding your fabric in half, selvage to selvage. Fold it in half a second time, matching the fold to the selvages.

> **HINT:** Instead of wrestling with long lengths of fabric (more than a yard and a half, or so), I estimate how much I need and cut off a piece that is slightly longer. For instance, if I need to cut six 2 1/2" wide strips, I'll cut off a half yard, press it, and use that for cutting the strips.

After folding the fabric in preparation for strip cutting, square off one end, removing the uneven edge. Rotate your mat a half turn or walk to the opposite side of the table to begin cutting the strips. Don't turn only the fabric. That will distort the even edge.

Let's assume that you need to cut many worms (you know, 2 1/2" wide strips). Most of you will line up the 2 1/2" line of a ruler with the square edge of the fabric, and cut a strip. Then, you will move the ruler off the strip, move the strip, reposition the ruler to cut the next strip, move the ruler off the strip, move the strip, etc. After doing this four or five times, you will check your strip and find that there are bends in it that make the strip resemble a "W". So, back to the beginning (and the other side of the table) to square the edge again. The reason that strips have these bends at the folds is that the edge from which you are measuring gets "out of square" from having the ruler tilted an unnoticeable amount with each cut. These tilts compound and cause crooked strips.

Instead of that old routine, consider this: Using your 15" ruler, you can cut six 2 1/2" strips very quickly and more accurately. Start by placing the 15" line of the ruler on the squared edge of the folded fabric. You now have six 2 1/2" strips under your ruler. Granted, the fabric is not cut into strips yet, but it will be in a minute.

Don't move any of the fabric or strips as you cut them. This is just wasted motion. With the vertical 15" line of the ruler on the squared edge of the fabric and any of the horizontal lines of the ruler along the lower fold of the fabric, cut. See figure 1 below. This results in a very square cut and enough fabric under the ruler to cut the six 2 1/2" wide strips.

Next, slide the ruler to the left until the 12 1/2" line is on the squared end of the fabric. That exposes a 2 1/2" strip of fabric between the cut you just made and the edge of the ruler. Make sure that a horizontal line of the ruler is still along the lower fold of the fabric and cut. See figure 2 on the next page.

Slide the ruler to the left another 2 1/2" inches and align the 10" line with the squared end of the fabric. Another 2 1/2" of fabric has been exposed. Check to see that a horizontal line is on the lower fold of the fabric and cut. See figure 3 on the next page.

Continue sliding the ruler to the left 2 1/2" at a time and making cuts until all six strips have been cut. At that time, stack and remove the cut strips. If you need more strips for your project, repeat these steps until all the strips are cut. There should be no need to square and straighten the end of the fabric unless you disturb it while repositioning it on the cutting mat.

Use this method even when you are cutting fewer strips. Start with a different line. For example, if you have only eight inches of fabric remaining, align the 7 1/2" line with the squared edge of the fabric. There are three uncut 2 1/2" wide strips under your ruler. Cut along the edge of the ruler. After cutting, move the ruler 2 1/2" to the left to the 5" line, for the second cut, and so on.

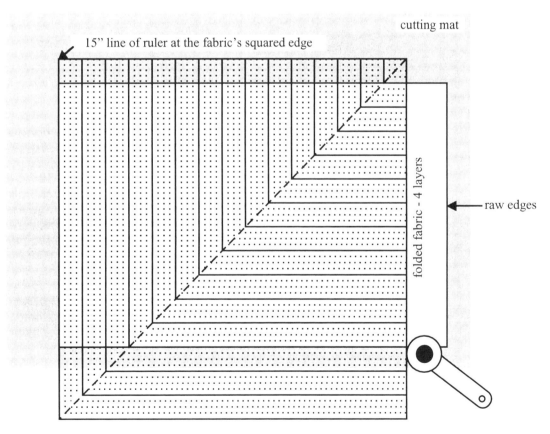

cutting mat

15" line of ruler at the fabric's squared edge

folded fabric - 4 layers

raw edges

fig. 1

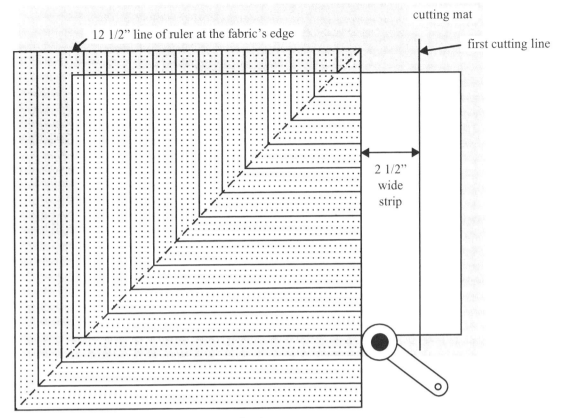

fig. 2

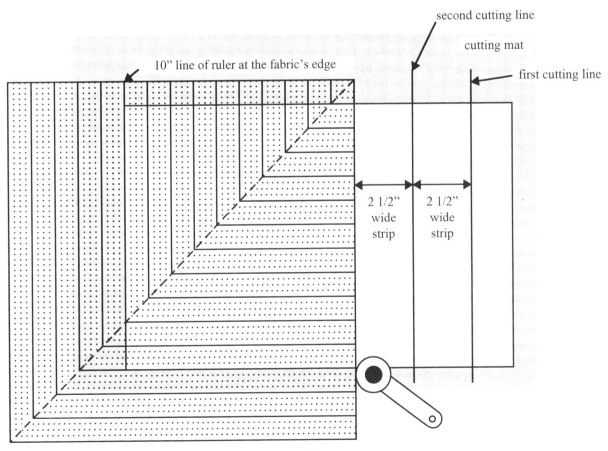

fig. 3

8

Take the time to list your "target numbers". For the 2 1/2" wide strips your target numbers were 15", 12 1/2", 10", 7 1/2", 5", and 2 1/2".

Consider another example. Let's say that for another project you need to cut strips that are 2 1/4" wide. Make a chart of your target numbers (multiples of 2 1/4") that reads as such: 13 1/2", 11 1/4", 9", 6 3/4", 4 1/2", and 2 1/4".

This means that when you align the ruler with the squared edge of the fabric to make your first cut, you will use the 13 1/2" line. Thirteen and a half inches will yield six 2 1/4" strips. Continue cutting as directed for the 2 1/2" wide strips, but use the target numbers from above so that you are cutting 2 1/4" wide strips.

This same principle of cutting can be applied to crosscutting strips into squares and rectangles. Figure 4 at the bottom of this page demonstrates cutting a 2 1/2" strip into 2 1/2" squares.

To do so, open the folded strip to two layers instead of four. If you feel brave enough, neatly stack four folded strips on top of each other so that you can cut through eight layers at a time. Trim the selvages, squaring that end. Continue to cut the strip(s) into squares as previously directed for cutting strips.

Use this method of cutting for cross-cutting strip pieced panels, such as those in the *Cobblestones* quilt on page 32. It will save lots of time and improve your precision.

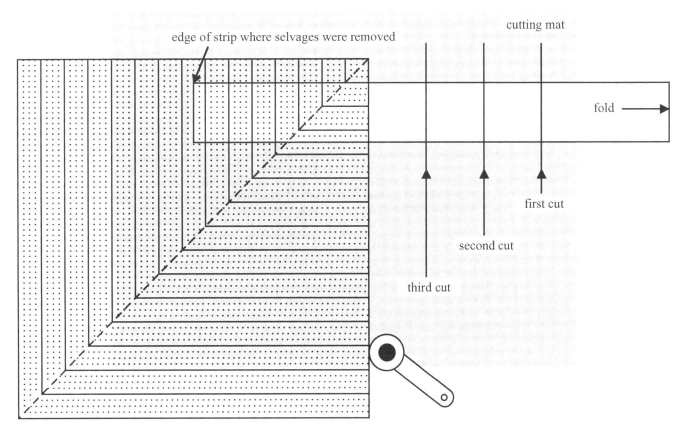

fig. 4

Cutting Triangles and Trapezoids

The reason that these quilt patterns, which contain half-square triangles and quarter-square triangles, can be constructed from nothing more than 2 1/2" wide strips is that the triangles are cut using tools or templates that are designed to fit the strips while perfectly adding the seam allowances. My preferred tools are the two Omnigrid triangles.

The Omnigrid triangles have the seam allowances built into them. In other words, if you use the Omnigrid 96 to cut a half-square triangle from a 2 1/2" strip by aligning the 2" measurement with the edge of the strip, as shown in photo #1 at the right, the triangle will measure 2" on each of the short sides when the quilt is finished. More on this will be discussed later in this section.

Omnigrid 96 and 96L

The Omnigrid 96 and the 96L are two sizes of the same tool. The 96L is larger. Both are used for cutting half-square triangles. I find the Omnigrid triangles very user friendly for both right-handed and left-handed quilters.

Half-square triangles have bias on the long diagonal side and straight of grain on the two short sides. Notice that the grid markings on the tool correspond to the grain lines. This should help you remember what the triangle does.

Omnigrid 96 triangle

Use this tool for cutting half-square triangles and trapezoids that have one square end.

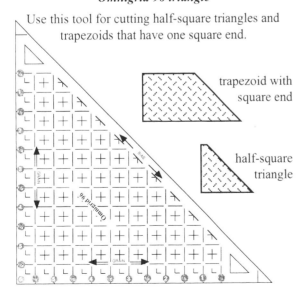

trapezoid with square end

half-square triangle

The Easy Angle tool, and perhaps some other tools, may be substituted for the Omnigrid 96. If you don't have a triangle tool that will do the job, use the templates on page 75. See photo #9 on page 13 for hints to make template use simple.

If you are using a triangle other than the Omnigrid, it is important that you lay the tool on the template (page 75) that is specified in the quilt pattern. For instance, if the pattern requires a 4" trapezoid, and you are using and Easy Angle tool, the template will align with the 4 1/2" marking, which is the bottom edge of the tool. When using the Omnigrid 96, the template will align with the 4" marking. The tools were designed by different people so they are used in slightly different ways. When in doubt, lay your tool on the template to check which markings to use.

To cut half-square triangles from the 2 1/2" wide strips, open one fold of the strip so that you are cutting through two layers, trim away the selvages, and align the 2" line on the Omnigrid 96 on the bottom of the strip, as shown in photo #1. Cut along the diagonal.

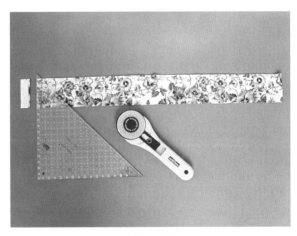

photo #1

Notice that the triangle has a flat tip on one corner. It is just missing the dog ear that would have been there if the triangle had been cut from a 2 7/8" square, as you usually do when rotary cutting half-square triangles.

Rotate the triangle into position to cut the next triangle. See photo #2 on the next page. Don't flip the Omnigrid 96 over to the backside. Keep it front side up.

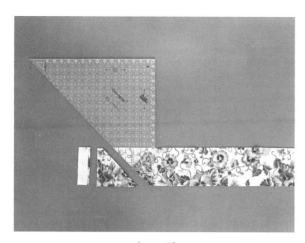

photo #2

Continue to rotate the triangle, aligning the 2" line with the edge of the strip, and cut as many half-square triangles as necessary for the pattern (photo #3). **Remember that you are cutting through a folded strip and each cut yields two triangles.**

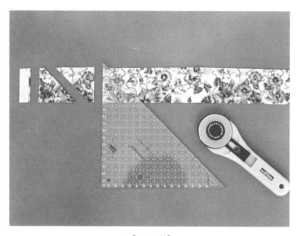

photo #3

Trapezoids are cut just as simply as the triangles. The only difference is the line that you align with the edge of the strip.

A *trapezoid* is any four sided shape that has two parallel sides and two other sides that are not parallel. Only two sizes of trapezoids are used in the patterns in this book. They are 4" and 6". Those sizes mean the finished length of the longest side of the shape.

These trapezoids have a direction. Some patterns require that trapezoids are cut all in the same direction, while others require that you cut an equal number of reverse pieces.

If the pattern requires reverse pieces, cut through folded strips as directed for the half-square triangles. If, however, all pieces need to be the same, be sure to open the strips to a single layer and place the strip right side up. Use the triangle tool in exactly the position shown in photo #4, or use the template right side up.

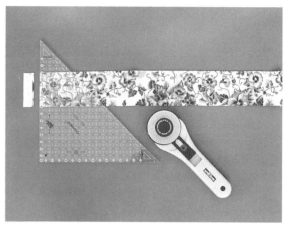

photo #4

To cut 4" (finished measurement of the long side) trapezoids, align the 4" marking on the Omnigrid 96 with the edge of the 2 1/2" strip, as shown in photo #4. cut along the diagonal.

Rotate the triangle tool and place the 4" marking along the top edge of the strip, as shown in photo #5. Cut.

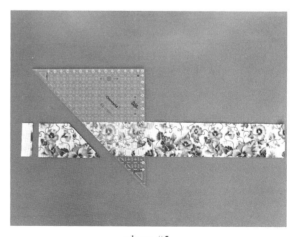

photo #5

Continue rotating the Omnigrid 96 and cutting until you have enough pieces for your pattern. See photo #6 on the next page.

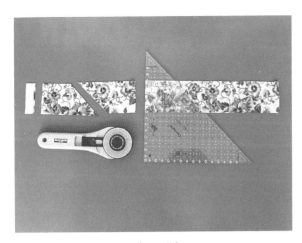

photo #6

Omnigrid 98 and 98L

The Omnigrid 98 and the 98L are two sizes of the same tool, but they do a different job than the 96's. The 98 and 98L are used for cutting quarter-square triangles. If you haven't yet purchased one, I strongly recommend that you purchase the larger one. Either will work for all of the patterns in this book, but the larger one will be more versatile once you begin to use it for other applications.

Quarter-square triangles have the bias on the two short sides and straight of grain on the long side. Once again, the grid markings on the tool correspond to the grain lines.

The Companion Angle tool, and perhaps some other tools, may be substituted for the Omnigrid 98. If you don't have a tool that will do the job, use template A on page 75. See photo #9 on page 13 for hints to make template use simple.

If you are using a triangle other than the Omnigrid, it is important that you lay the tool on template A (page 75) to see which line to use. The reason has been explained earlier in the section about the Omnigrid 96.

To cut quarter-square triangles from the 2 1/2" wide strips, open one fold of the strip so that you will cut through two layers. Place the tool in position, as shown in photo #7, aligning the 4" measurement with the bottom edge of the strip. ***The 4" line is the one directly below the number 4 on the tool.*** Cut along both edges of the triangle.

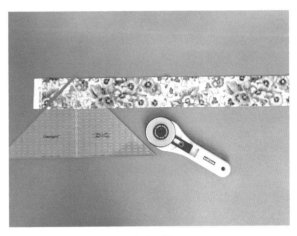

photo #7

Rotate the triangle tool and place the 4" marking along the top edge of the strip, as shown in photo #8. Cut. Continue cutting until you have enough quarter-square triangles for your quilt pattern.

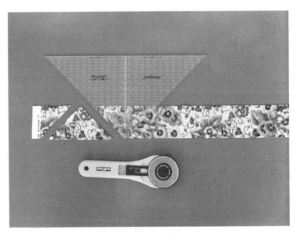

photo #8

Omnigrid 98 triangle

Use this tool for cutting quarter-square triangles.

quarter-square
triangle

You will notice that the top of the quarter-square triangle is slightly flattened. Once again, it is just missing a tiny dog ear.

Using the Templates

When using templates, I take the easy way out. I use a copy machine or my computer to make templates. ***Be sure to compare copies to the original!!! Many copiers greatly distort and your templates may be incorrect.***

Tape the template to the underside of any suitable tool that you have using double sided tape. See photo #9. I prefer a temporary adhesive. Check for it at your local craft or office supply store. Use these set-ups just as you would the Omnigrid triangles.

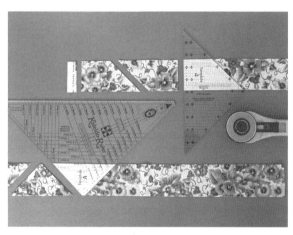

photo #9

More Tips for Cutting

I like to cut through as many as eight layers at a time to speed up the process. One example is the way that I cut trapezoids for the *Friendship Braid* pattern.

The *Friendship Braid* requires an equal number of light and dark pieces. In addition, it requires an equal number of reverse trapezoids in both values. So, I open two light and two dark strips to a single fold, and carefully stack them with the selvages all on top of one another and the folds at the other end. See photo #10. Now I'll be cutting equal numbers of light trapezoids, light reverse-trapezoids, dark trapezoids, and dark reverse-trapezoids. Doing this thirteen more times will cut the entire quilt in short order.

Use these tools to cut pieces that use templates in other books. Lay the tool on the template to see which line to use, or use the template method described at the left.

Trimming the Dog Ears

Aligning the half-square triangles and trapezoids is much more accurate if you take the time to trim the dog ears as you cut the pieces instead of after they are sewn. You will find that this is a time saver, too.

To trim the dog ears from the half-square triangles, stack as many as eight pieces neatly atop one another. Align the 2 1/2" line of a straight ruler (not one of the triangles) with the edge of the triangles and trim the dog ears. Trim the trapezoids the same way except use the 4 1/2" or 6 1/2" line, depending upon the size of the piece. See the sketches below.

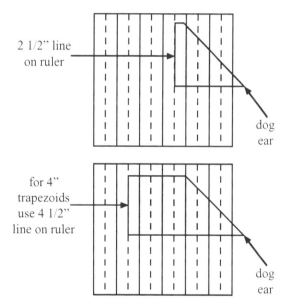

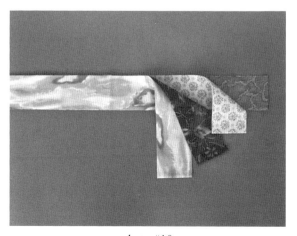

photo #10

Sewing Precision

The success of your quilts depends upon precise seam allowances. *I cannot stress this point enough.* Don't believe the person who tells you that as long as you are consistent, it will be okay. That only works for some quilts, like *Stacked Coins, Cobblestones*, and similar ones. Quilts that have areas of many seams as well as other areas with few seams must be constructed with accurate seam allowances. If you haven't checked your seam allowances in the past, do so before beginning by performing the following test.

Test: From scraps cut four rectangles that measure 1 1/2" x 4 1/2". Sew them together along the long edges using a scant 1/4" seam allowance. This is about a needle's width narrower than a true 1/4". Press the seam allowances to one side. The finished piece should measure 4 1/2" square. If not, adjust your seam allowance and repeat the test.

Finished sample will measure 4 1/2" square

Borders

Whenever possible, the outer border strips should be cut with the lengthwise grain in the long direction. This will keep them from stretching and rippling. The yardage requirements allow for lengthwise grain borders. It is not necessary that narrow inner borders be cut along the lengthwise grain.

My solution to accurately cutting long, lengthwise grain border strips and sashing strips, such as those used in the *Stacked Coins, Friendship Braid*, and *Cobblestones* quilts is solved in one word -- tear! This is recommended for 100% cotton fabrics, only. Test fabrics of other fiber content before tearing the yardage.

Fabrics are woven with the strong warp yarns running in the lengthwise direction and the weaker weave yarns in the crosswise direction. This is the very reason why the fabric doesn't stretch along the lengthwise grain while having a good deal of give on the crosswise grain. When tearing across the width of fabrics, you are breaking the stronger yarns. This leads to snags and weakening of the fabric beyond the 1/4" seam allowances.

On the other hand, when tearing fabric along its length, you are breaking the weak yarns and tearing parallel to the warp yarns. The result is a much smoother edge and a perfectly straight, on-grain border strip.

If you are unsure about how well your fabric will tear, start by tearing off a selvage. Clip one end of the fabric 1" away from the selvage edge. Tear this selvage off. Don't be timid. Pull firmly and rather quickly. What do you think of the edge? Press the torn edge. How does it look now? If it is satisfactory, you are ready to tear the borders.

Lay an end of the border fabric flat on a table. Measure the desired cut width of your border from the edge where you have removed the selvage. See the sketch below. Make a clip at this point on the end of the fabric just as you did when removing the selvage. Measure from this first clip and make a second clip for the second border. Repeat to mark all four borders. Tear!

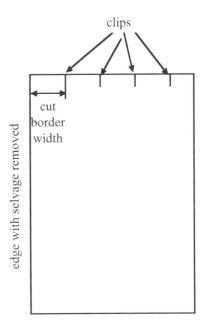

Press the border strips. I prewash my fabrics before piecing a quilt. I don't press the border fabric until it is torn into strips. What a timesaver that is. It is so much simpler to press a narrow strip of fabric than it is to press yards of the full width.

Measuring and easing are important steps. Without them your quilt may be different lengths on opposite sides and will not be square. Be sure the quilt is pressed well before measuring it. As you are measuring, keep the quilt top fairly taut on a flat surface. The quilt top contains many seams, and they each have a slight amount of slack where the seam allowances are pressed to the side. Conversely, the borders have few or no seams and are cut along the stable, lengthwise grain. Therefore, keeping the quilt taut while measuring is imperative, but do not stretch quilts that are set on point.

Borders can be applied with either overlapped or mitered corners. *If you choose to miter the borders for any of the quilts in these patterns, purchase an additional half yard of border fabric.* The amount of fabric allowed is for overlapped borders.

Overlapped corners

Find the length of the quilt. Measure in several places to determine the average length. Take measurements along seam lines and in areas that go through the centers of the blocks, but not along the outside edges. Cut two border strips 1/2" wider than the desired finished width of the border by the average measured length of the quilt. Pin them to the sides of the quilt, matching the center points and ends of the quilt and borders. Continue pinning the borders to the quilt easing, if necessary. Sew. Press the seam allowances toward the borders.

Now, determine the width of the quilt, measuring in several places, as before. Include the additional width created by the side borders. Cut two border strips to fit (finished border width plus 1/2" x width of quilt) and pin them to the top and bottom of the quilt as you did the side borders. Sew. Press the seam allowances toward the borders.

If you are adding more than one border, repeat the above steps for each one.

quilt with overlapped borders

Mitered corners

None of the quilts in this book have mitered corners in their directions, but it is important information. Since you are challenged to be inspired to personalize these designs to fit your needs, you may want to miter the corners of the borders.

Determine both the width and length of your quilt. To calculate how long to cut your borders, add two times the border width plus an inch or two to the measurements of your quilt. If the quilt will have more than one border with mitered corners, sew the borders together into a panel before attaching them.

Even with mitered corners you can square your quilt. Put a pin at the center of each border. Measure half the length of your quilt in each direction from the center pin and mark those points with pins. Now, pin the border to your quilt, matching the pins with the center and ends of the quilt. Use additional pins as needed.

Attach borders to two opposite sides of the quilt first. Begin and end the stitching on the seam line, 1/4" from the edge of the quilt top. Backstitch at each end. Press the seam allowances toward the borders. Repeat with the remaining two border pieces.

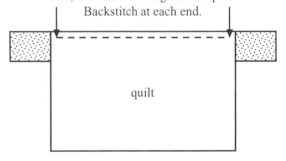

Begin and end stitching on the seam line, 1/4" from the edge of the quilt. Backstitch at each end.

quilt

Place a corner of the quilt on the ironing board. See below. Lay the vertical border on the ironing board first. Lay the horizontal border over it, as shown.

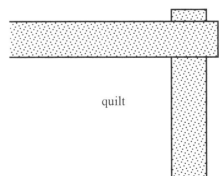

quilt

Tuck the end of the horizontal border under so that the fold makes a 45 degree angle. Press. Lay a ruler on top of this corner to check that it is square and the angle is accurate. If your border is strip pieced, make sure the seam lines match.

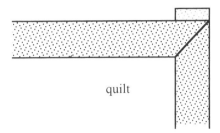

Place the borders right sides together and pin. Match the seam lines if the borders have more than one fabric. Stitch on the pressed crease, starting on the seam line, being careful not to catch the quilt top in the stitching. Stitch to the outer edge of the border. Check your work. Make sure you are pleased with the finished corner before doing any trimming. If it is correct, trim the excess fabric, leaving 1/4" for seam allowances. Press the seam allowances to one side or open. Repeat this process for all four corners.

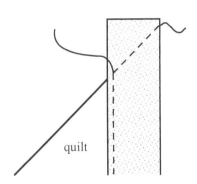

Place the borders right sides together and stitch on the pressed crease, starting on the seam line. Be careful not to catch the quilt top in the stitching.

Quilting and Binding

These are basic skills that have books and classes dedicated solely to them. Almost every quilting magazine on the market contains basic instruction for quilting and binding in every issue. Take advantage of demonstrations and classes that are available to you. The quilting and binding are highly visible and are a part of every quilt. Learn to do them well.

If you need more detailed information for binding than what is given below, *Happy Endings* by Mimi Dietrich, published by That Patchwork Place, is a good reference.

After quilting, trim the excess batting and backing in preparation for binding. I use a 1/2" wide binding. Many quilts have pieced edges, and therefore, have only 1/4" seam allowances. To allow for the 1/2" binding, trim the backing and batting, leaving an additional 1/4" beyond the raw edge of the quilt top. This will create the necessary 1/2" seam allowance.

For a 1/2" double binding, cut cross-grain strips 3 1/4" wide. Bias strips are only necessary for binding curves, although, some fabrics, like plaids and stripes, make a more interesting binding when cut on the bias. Cut enough strips to go around the perimeter of your quilt. Sew them together, end on end, and press the seam allowances open. Press the strip in half, wrong sides together, lengthwise.

Sew the binding to the quilt with 1/2" seam allowances, aligning the raw edges of the binding with the cut edge of the quilt. Start in the middle of one side, leaving the first six inches of binding unsewn. Stitch, stopping 1/2" from the corner. Lift your presser foot and pull the quilt out a few inches from under the machine to fold the binding. It is not necessary to clip the threads. Rotate the quilt a quarter turn, counterclockwise. Fold the binding up and away, creating a 45 degree angle. Then, fold the binding back down toward you.

Begin stitching at the edge of the quilt. Continue stitching down the second side, stopping 1/2" from the corner. Miter this corner as you did the first one and continue around the quilt. After you have mitered the last corner, stop stitching 12" from where you first began to attach the binding.

Trim the excess binding, leaving 1/2" for seam allowances. Stitch the two ends of the binding together. Press the seam allowances open. Finish stitching this section of the binding to the quilt.

Push the binding to the back of the quilt and pin in place. The folded edge of the binding should just cover the stitching line. Fold the corners into neat miters on the back of the quilt. Hand stitch the binding into place.

Star Sampler -- 47" x 56 1/2"

Quilted by Debbie Caffrey

Sister's Choice -- 62" x 74"

Quilted by Mary Johnson of Sutton, Alaska

Square Knots -- 51 1/2" x 60"

Pieced by Erin Caffrey
Quilted by Mary Johnson of Sutton, Alaska

Road to Oklahoma -- 64" x 80"

Quilted by Karen Tomczak of Anchorage, Alaska

Four on Point -- 51" x 62"

Quilted by Karen Tomczak of Anchorage, Alaska

Four Patches & Friends Mystery -- 60" x 76"

Pieced and quilted by Dottie Tessandore of Anchorage, Alaska

Four Patches & Friends -- 68" x 84"

Quilted by Karen Tomczak of Anchorage, Alaska

Trees -- 60" x 80"

Quilted by Mary Johnson of Sutton, Alaska

Buzz Saw -- 60" x 72"

Quilted by Debbie Caffrey

Friendship Braid -- 67" x 82"

Quilted by Norma Kindred of Eagle River, Alaska

Cobblestones -- 67" x 82"

Quilted by Norma Kindred of Eagle River, Alaska

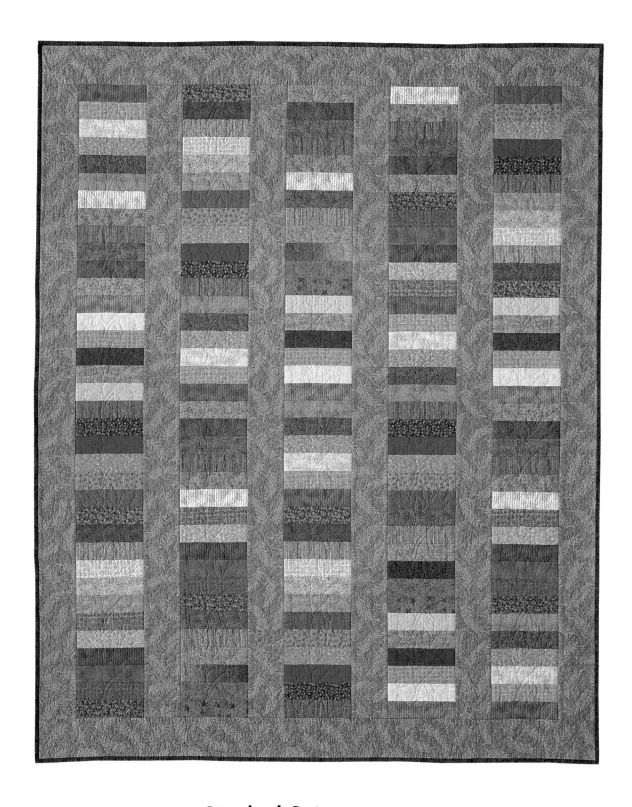

Stacked Coins -- 66" x 81"

Quilted by Norma Kindred of Eagle River, Alaska

Stacked Coins

The size of the quilt shown on page 28 is 66" x 81".

Fabric Requirements

When selecting the strips, I chose to use mostly medium values with an occasional light or dark strip for interest. This quilt is also known as *Bars*.

36 worms	
Sashing & borders	**2 1/4 yards**
Binding	**3/4 yard**
Backing	**5 yards**

Piecing

Sew the thirty-six strips into six panels of six strips each. Press the seam allowances to one side.

Trim the selvages from one end of the panels and crosscut each of them into five equal sections. Measure the shortest strip that you have used and divide its usable length by five to determine how wide to crosscut the sections.

> **For example:** If the shortest strip in your panels is 40" long, you should crosscut all of the panels 8" wide. On the other hand, if your shortest strip is 42 1/2" long, you can crosscut your panels into 8 1/2" wide sections.

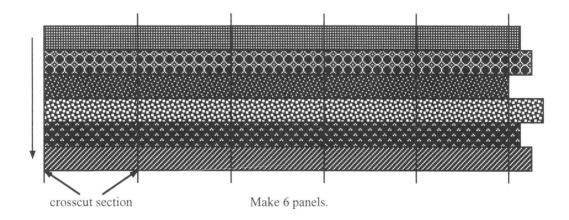

crosscut section   Make 6 panels.

Randomly position the crosscut sections, rotating some of them upside down, and sew them into five rows of six sections. Refer to the photo on page 28 or the graphic on page 31. Press.

To add the borders and sashing, measure the length of your rows and determine their average length. ***Do not just sew the pieces on and trim to fit.*** Your quilt will be much more square if you follow the instructions on the next page.

Remove the selvages from your sashing/border fabric. Cut it lengthwise into four 5" wide strips and four 5 1/4" wide strips. Reserve two of the 5 1/4" strips for the top and bottom borders. Trim the remaining six pieces to the measurement of the average length of your rows.

Pin the sashes and borders to the pieced rows, matching the centers and ends, easing as necessary to fit. The two wider pieces are the side borders and go along the outside edges of the quilt.

> NOTE: The border strips are cut slightly wider than the sashes to allow for the edge of the quilt to be bound with a 1/2" wide binding and still be 4 1/2" wide like the sashes when finished.

Sew the rows, sashes, and side borders together. Press all seam allowances toward the sashes and borders.

Measure the width of the quilt in several places to determine its average width. Trim the remaining two borders to fit. Pin them to the top and bottom edges of the quilt and stitch. Press the seam allowances toward the borders.

Options to Consider --

For a full/queen size quilt, make the quilt seven rows wide instead of five. Piece nine panels of seven strips per panel. Each of the seven rows contains forty-two "coins" (six sections of seven coins). This will require sixty-three worms. For the sashing and borders, you will need two lengths, about five yards, of fabric.

Use this technique to make a piano keys border for other quilts. See the *Sister's Choice* quilt on page 18.

Whether you are making a *Stacked Coins* quilt or a piano keys border, try sewing random widths of strips together when piecing the panels. This is a great way to use your "strings" of fabric no matter how wide they are.

The *Stacked Coins* quilt in the graphic below uses a variation of the strip sashing setting used in the one shown in the photograph on page 28. For this setting, remove the selvages from the setting fabric, as described on page 30. Then, cut four narrow sashes 2 1/2" wide and four border strips 7 1/2" wide. Complete the quilt as directed for the first variation.

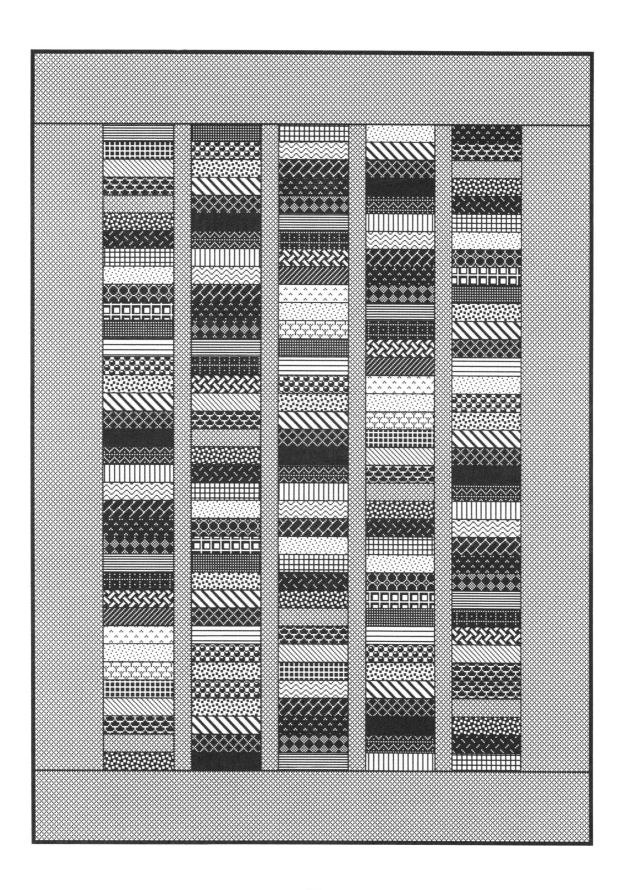

Cobblestones

The size of the quilt shown on page 27 is 67" x 82".

Fabric Requirements

Another name for this traditional quilt is *Garden Path*. It is most effective when the "cobblestone" fabrics are similar in value. Extreme differences in values will cause a checkerboard effect. To make your quilt like the one shown on page 27, choose a light control color for the strips that make the triangles along the edges of the rows. If desired, you could use just one light fabric for all of the light strips.

40 medium to dark worms for cobblestones

16 light worms to be used for strip piecing triangles on edges of rows *plus* --

Thirty 2 1/2" squares of light fabric. These will be used for making the corner sections of the rows. Cut these from at least several different fabrics unless you are using only one light.

Sashing & borders	2 1/4 yards
Binding	3/4 yard
Backing	5 yards

Piecing

Sew the strips into eight panels of seven strips each. Each panel will have a light strip on the top and another on the bottom with five medium to dark strips between them. Press the seam allowances to one side, all in the same direction.

Trim the selvages from one end of the panels and crosscut each of them into 2 1/2" wide sections. You will use 120 sections to make the quilt shown on page 27.

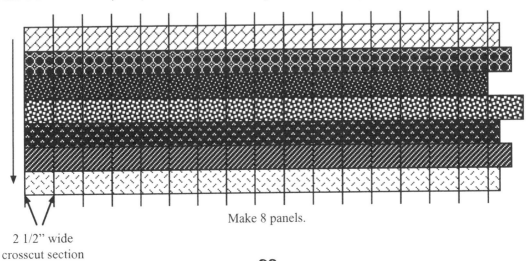

Make 8 panels.

2 1/2" wide
crosscut section

Use ten crosscut sections and the thirty 2 1/2" squares of light to make ten corner units. To start, remove the third square of all ten sections as shown in figure 1, and set it aside for another use.

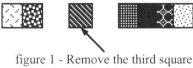 

figure 1 - Remove the third square from ten crosscut sections.

figure 2 - Make 10 of each.

Sew a light square to each of the short sections from figure 1 above. See figure 2. Press the seam allowances to one side.

Arrange the sections from above with the remaining ten 2 1/2" squares to complete the ten corner units. See figure 3. Press the seam allowances in the direction shown by the arrow.

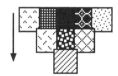

figure 3 - Make 10

Sew the remaining crosscut sections into five rows, twenty-two sections per row. Some tips for making the rows are:

Start by sewing the sections into pairs like those in figure 4. The top of the section on the right extends 1/4" above the first seam line of the section on the left. This makes the bottom of the section on the left extend 1/4" below the bottom seam line of the section on the right. To do this, follow the instructions below.

figure 4

Place a crosscut section on the bottom, right side up, with the pressed seam allowances going downward. Place a second section on top of the first, right sides together, with the pressed seam allowances going upward. Shift the section on top down two inches and match all the seam lines so that the sections are positioned like those shown in figure 4 and described above. Do this consistently and all of the pairs will be positioned correctly with their seam allowances going in the right directions to complete the construction of the rows.

Press the seam allowances to one side.

Sew eleven pairs together, shifting the top section down 2" and matching the seam lines as before to make a row. See figure 5 to get started. Press the seam allowances to one side. Continue sewing sections together to make five long rows.

Add a corner unit to both ends of all five rows. The finished rows should look like the one shown in figure 6 on the next page.

figure 5

Make sure the rows are pressed well before trimming them. Trim the points from all four sides of the rows by aligning the 1/4" line of your rotary cutting ruler with the finished corners of the outer cobblestones. See the placement of the cutting lines in the lower section of figure 6 on the next page.

Measure the rows to determine their average length. Get a good measurement, but be careful not to stretch the rows as you measure. Because they are set on point, the bias makes it more challenging to get an accurate measurement. Therefore, it is even more important to get an average measurement for cutting the sashings in order to keep your quilt square and flat.

Follow the instructions for the *Stacked Coins* quilt on pages 30 and 31 for adding sashing and border strips. Use either option -- sashings and borders of equal widths or narrow sashings with wider borders.

Options to Consider --

For a full/queen size quilt, make the quilt seven rows wide instead of five. Make the rows a few sections longer. This size will use about thirteen strip pieced panels and forty-two 2 1/2" squares of light fabric. To make thirteen panels you will need sixty-five medium to dark worms and twenty-six light worms. For the sashing and borders, you will need two lengths, about five yards, of fabric. As always, these are ballpark figures. You may only want six rows of cobblestones and borders of your choosing.

Another option for making a full/queen is to complete the smaller quilt, as directed, and then add a wide border as shown in the graphic on the next page.

Wouldn't one of these rows make a great border, too? The outer edge will need to be stay stitched or have another border attached to control the bias edge. It will take a little designing to piece this border, so I would recommend it only for experienced quilters. A tip for adding complicated pieced borders is to piece the border slightly larger than needed for the quilt. Then, insert a narrow plain border between the quilt top and the pieced border to make them fit together. See figure 7.

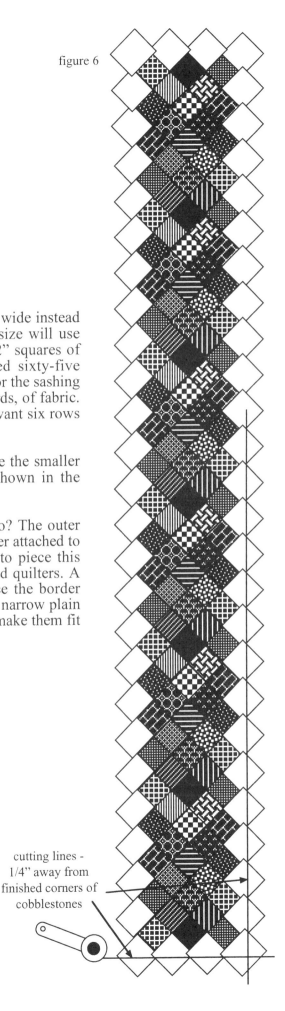

figure 6

figure 7

cutting lines -
1/4" away from
finished corners of
cobblestones

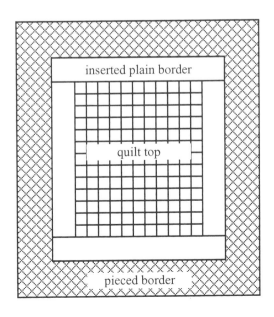

34

One way to make the *Cobblestones* quilt larger without piecing more rows is to add a wide border. With the addition of 10" wide borders, the quilt shown below will be approximately 87" x 102".

The *Stacked Coins* and *Friendship Braid* quilts on pages 28 and 26, respectively, can be simply enlarged by adding an additional border, too.

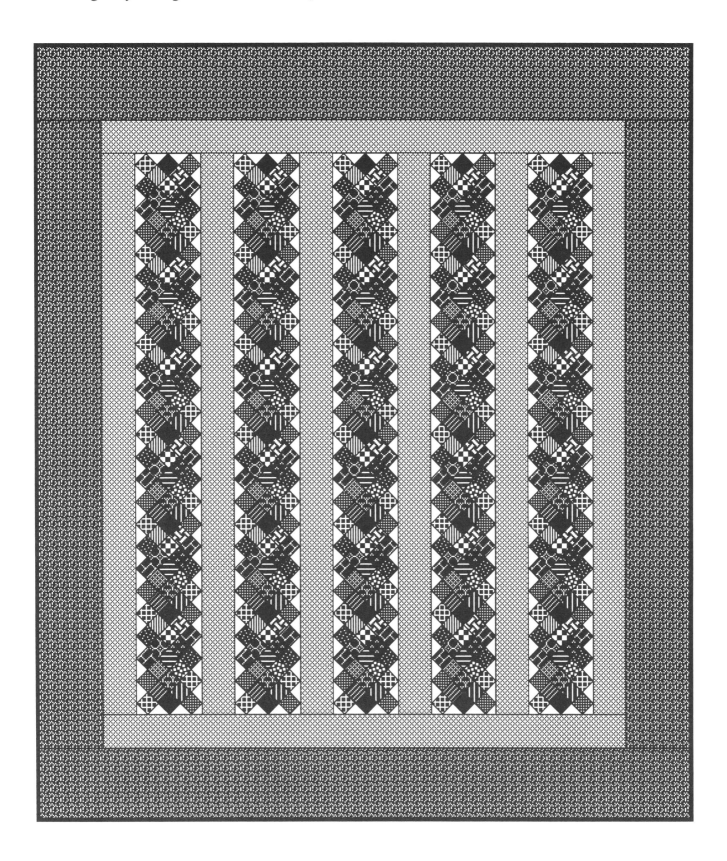

Square Knots

The size of the quilt shown on page 19 is 51 1/2" x 60".

Fabric Requirements

I couldn't find this block in any of my reference materials. However, how can you claim such a simple variation of a nine patch an original block? I'm sure it must have been pieced by quilters who have come many years before me. Because I am very fond of the Churn Dash block, I am taken with this simplified version, too. It makes a great baby quilt or small lap quilt. With the optional setting that is given at the end of the pattern, it could be used for a larger quilt.

15 Worms - Each strip will make two blocks.
Erin used thirty worms, doubled the other yardages, and made two quilts so that the fabrics in the blocks were not repeated.

Background and setting squares	1 1/2 yards
Border and setting triangles	1 3/4 yards
Binding	3/4 yard
Backing	3 1/4 yards

Cutting

Worms

From each strip cut eight 2 1/2" squares and eight 1 1/2" x 2 1/2" rectangles.

Background and setting squares

Cut four 6 1/2" wide strips.
    Cut these strips into twenty 6 1/2" squares.

Cut seven 2 1/2" wide strips.
    Cut these strips into thirty 2 1/2" squares and 120 rectangles that are 1 1/2" x 2 1/2".

Border, side triangles, and corner triangles

Split the 1 3/4 yard piece in half, lengthwise. Reserve one half for borders.

From the second half --

Cut five 9 3/4" squares.
    Cut these squares twice, diagonally, to make four quarter-square triangles from each.   Yield: 20 triangles

Cut two 5 1/8" squares.
    Cut these squares once, diagonally, to make two half-square triangles from each.   Yield: 4 triangles

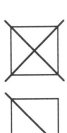

Piecing

Sew each 1 1/2" x 2 1/2" rectangle of the worm fabrics to a background rectangle of the same size. Chain piece. Press the seam allowances toward the darker fabric.

Make 8 from each worm fabric.

Arrange the pieced units from above with the 2 1/2" squares of worm and background fabrics to make thirty Square Knots blocks.

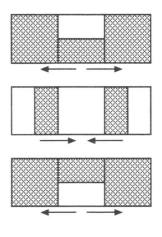

Sew the pieces into horizontal rows. Press the seam allowances of the top and bottom rows away from the center unit. Press the seam allowances of the middle row toward the center square.

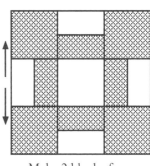

Sew the rows together and press the seam allowances away from the middle row.

Make 2 blocks from each worm fabric.

Arrange the blocks on point, alternating them with the 6 1/2" setting squares as shown on the next page. Place the quarter-square triangles around the outer edges. There will be two triangles left over. The four half-square triangles are the corners of the quilt.

Sew the quilt top together by making diagonal rows. The bold diagonal lines in the graphic on the next page define the diagonal rows. Sew corner and side triangles to the ends of their respective rows in the correct position. After sewing the blocks and triangles into diagonal rows, press the seam allowances away from the Square Knots blocks. Sew the rows together and press the seams to one side.

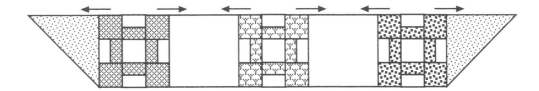

Cut the remaining fabric into four lengthwise panels that are 5" wide. Apply these borders with overlapped corners. See page 14 for more instruction on borders.

Options to Consider --

One way to enlarge the quilt is to put four blocks together, as shown at the top of the next page. Then, set the four block groups with wide sashings, which are cut 4 1/2" x 12 1/2" and 4 1/2" cornerstones.

When making this variation of the quilt, instead of piecing four blocks and sewing the Square Knots blocks together, as shown at the left, I would eliminate some seams and piece the block as shown below. Replace eight of the background 1 1/2" rectangles with four 2 1/2" squares. These squares are identified by the * symbol. Make five horizontal rows as shown by the bold lines. Press the seam allowances of each row so that the are opposite those seam allowances in the adjacent row.

Refer to the graphic on the next page for the suggested setting for this variation.

When setting the quilt with sashes, sew the blocks, sashes, and cornerstones into horizontal rows. Press the seam allowances of all rows toward the sashes.

Sew the rows together. Press the seam allowances toward the sashing rows.

Add borders as desired.

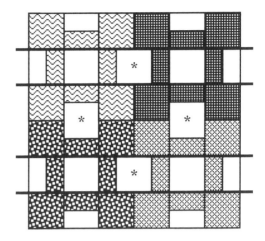

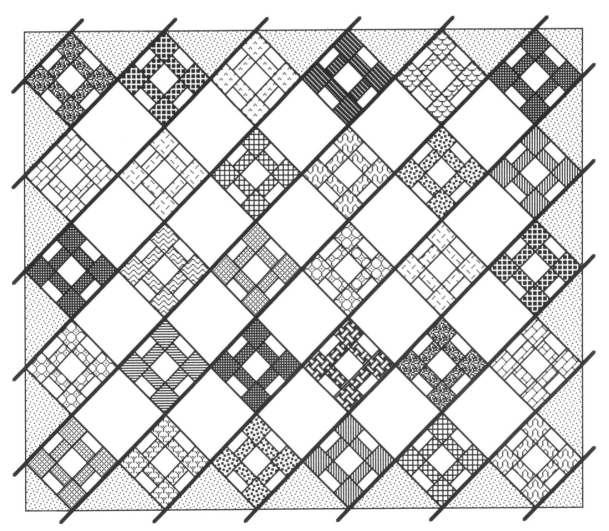

In order to save space, the quilt in the graphic above has been turned sideways.

The finished size of this variation with 8" wide borders is 68" x 84", a twin size. It allows for some great quilting space in the sashes, cornerstones, and borders.

Use twenty-four worms for this size. Other fabric yardages are:

Background	1 yard		Border	2 yards
Sashing	1 1/2 yards		Backing	5 yards
Cornerstones	1/2 yard		Binding	1 yard

Four Patches & Friends

The size of the quilt shown on page 23 is 68" x 84". Dottie Tessandore made a variation of this quilt, shown on page 22, during one of my mystery quilt workshops. Her quilt uses a main focus fabric in place of the large scale print fabrics, and demonstrates the fact that all of the patterns in this book are suitable for making quilts from yardage of fewer fabrics.

Fabric Requirements

When teaching my "Can of Worms" workshops, this is by far the most popular block and quilt in the group. It is so simple, but the settings are numerous. This is a great quilt pattern for making a quilt to commemorate graduation, a wedding, a family reunion, or for saying good-bye to someone dear.

40 large scale print worms	
20 small scale print worms	
Light background for signature area	2 1/2 yards
Narrow inner border and binding	1 1/2 yards
Backing	5 yards

Cutting

Worms

Cut sixteen 2 1/2" squares from each of the sixty worms.

Background

Cut eighteen 4 1/2" wide strips.
Cut these strips into 160 squares (4 1/2").

Narrow inner border

Cut eight 2 1/2" wide strips.
Cut these strips into four 2 1/2" x 34 1/2" strips,
four 2 1/2" x 32 1/2" strips, and
eight 2 1/2" x 8 1/2" rectangles.

Piecing

These instructions are for completing one 8" block. For each block you need:
two 4 1/2" squares of background,
eight 2 1/2" squares of one large scale print, and
four 2 1/2" squares of one small scale print.

Use four squares of the large scale print and the four squares of small scale print to make two four patch blocks. Press the seam allowances as shown by the arrows in the sketches at the right.

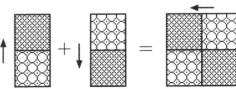

Make 2

Place a square of large scale print on two opposite corners of both 4 1/2" squares of background, right sides together. Stitch along the diagonal lines of the small squares, as shown by the dashed lines in figure 1. Flip up the corners to check your work. The finished units should look like the one in figure 2.

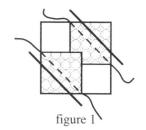

figure 1

If correct, trim the excess leaving 1/4" for seam allowances, as shown in figure 1 by the solid lines. Press the seam allowances toward the triangles.

Arrange the four patches and units from above to make a Four Patches & Friends block. Press the seam allowances as shown by the arrows. ***Be sure that the signature areas of the block form a diagonal through the block.*** This will allow you to layout your blocks in many different patterns like those used for log cabin quilts. See pages 42 through 44 for some variations of this quilt.

figure 2

Repeat to make eighty blocks.

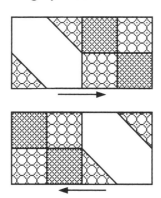

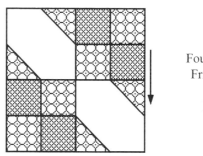

Four Patches & Friends block

Make 80

Arrange the blocks as shown in the graphic on page 42. Piece the forty-eight blocks of the center into a quilt top, making eight horizontal rows of six blocks. Press the seam allowances of the odd rows to the left. Press the seam allowances of the even rows to the right. Sew the rows together. Press the seam allowances to one side.

Piece the remaining blocks and 2 1/2" x 8 1/2" rectangles to make the four outer borders. See page 42.

Sew the 32 1/2" long strips into two narrow inner borders for the sides. Sew these and the outer borders into position on the sides. Press the seam allowances toward the inner borders.

Sew the 34 1/2" long strips together to make inner borders for the top and bottom of the quilt. Add them and the outer borders to the quilt. Press the seam allowances toward the inner borders.

Options to Consider --

For a full or queen size quilt, you may just add a wide border or two to this quilt. Otherwise, a queen size quilt without an additional border will require 120 blocks.

Making 120 blocks will use sixty large scale worms and thirty small scale worms. To design any other size quilt you would like, use this method for calculating the number of strips needed:
    One 4 1/2" wide strip of background fabric, two 2 1/2" wide large scale strips, and one 2 1/2" wide small scale strip will make four blocks.

Use sashing or other setting options to create an endless number of designs with this block. Using setting pieces, obviously, will enlarge the quilt without making more blocks.

This is an exploded view of the layout for the quilt shown on page 23. Consider some of the options shown on the next two pages, as well.

Each layout shown on this page and the next uses forty-eight Four Patches & Friends blocks.

Barn Raising

Zig Zag

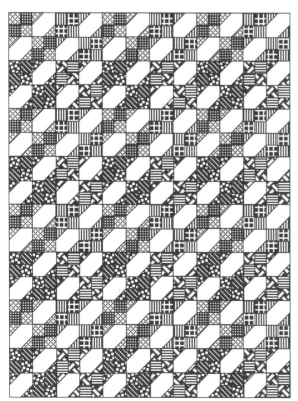

Fields & Furrows

Rambling Trails

Four Square
Make twenty Four Patch blocks for the cornerstones and
cut thirty-one 4 1/2" x 16 1/2" rectangles for the sashes.

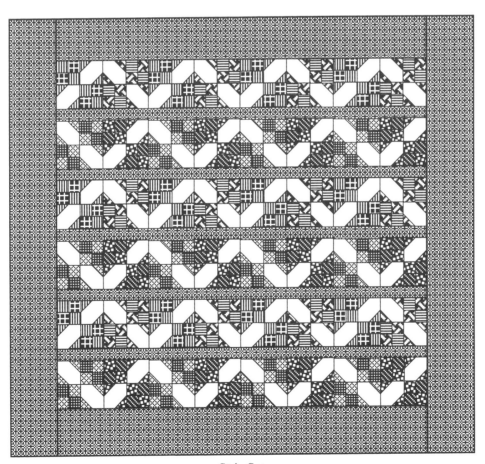

Strip Set
Refer to the directions for the *Stacked Coins* quilt for instructions on this setting.

Buzz Saw

The size of the quilt shown on page 25 is 60" x 72".

Fabric Requirements

This quilt can be made with many different light and dark fabrics, or use one or two control backgrounds and numerous accent fabrics that contrast with them as I have. Be sure to look at the Christmas package option on page 48. That effect was discovered by a quilter in a workshop in Austin, Texas.

120 rectangles of accent fabrics   **2 1/2" x 11"**
If you want to repeat your fabrics or make each saw blade from four blocks of the same accent fabric you will need thirty worms.

Light background	1 3/4 yards
Dark background	1 yard
Binding	3/4 yard
Backing	3 3/4 yards

Cutting -- Be sure you have read pages 10 through 13 before cutting!

Cutting the accent fabrics when using 120 rectangles -- 2 1/2" x 11"

All of the 2 1/2" x 11" rectangles will be cut in exactly the same way. Carefully stack as many rectangles as you feel comfortable cutting at one time. I cut eight layers at a time. *Be sure they are **all positioned right side up.*** You want ***no reverse pieces*** for this quilt.

Cut a 2 1/2" x 6 1/2" piece from one end of the stack of rectangles.

Place the 4" line of your Omnigrid 96 or template 4 on the stack of the 4 1/2" long rectangles that remain after cutting off the 6 1/2" piece. Cut a trapezoid. Don't be concerned that the trapezoid has a flat point. See figure 1 on the next page. All that is missing is the dog ear. You won't have to trim it later, and this flat tip will make the alignment of the pieces perfect!

Cutting the accent fabrics when using thirty 2 1/2" wide strips

Cut four 2 1/2" x 6 1/2" rectangles from each of the thirty strips.

Open the remaining parts of the strips to a single layer. You cannot use any reverse trapezoids in this pattern. Stack as many pieces as you feel comfortable cutting at one time. *Be sure they are **all positioned right side up.*** Cut four 4" (finished size) trapezoids from each fabric using the Omnigrid 96 or template 4. See the instructions on page 11 for more information on cutting trapezoids.

Cutting the Background

Light background

Cut twenty 2 1/2" wide strips.

Cut four 2 1/2" x 6 1/2" rectangles from each of the twenty strips.

Open the remaining parts of the strips to a single layer. You cannot use any reverse trapezoids in this pattern. Stack as many pieces as you feel comfortable cutting at one time. *Be sure they are all positioned right side up.* Cut four 4" (finished size) trapezoids from each strip remainder using the Omnigrid 96 or template 4. See the instructions on page 11 for more information on cutting trapezoids.

Dark background

Cut ten 2 1/2" wide strips.

Cut each strip into four 2 1/2" x 6 1/2" rectangles and four 4" (finished size) trapezoids, as directed above for the light background. You will have a total of forty rectangles and forty trapezoids.

For accurate alignment and less work later, trim the dog ears from the trapezoids that were <u>not</u> cut from the 11" long rectangles before starting to sew. See page 13 for more instruction.

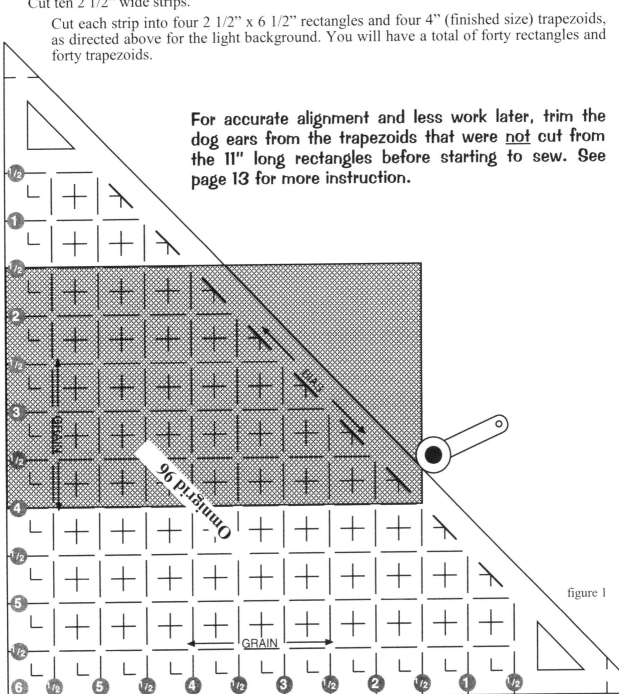

figure 1

46

Piecing

Each block is constructed with one 2 1/2" x 6 1/2" rectangle and one 4" trapezoid of an accent fabric *and* one 2 1/2" x 6 1/2" rectangle and one 4" trapezoid of a background fabric. Place the trapezoids, right sides together, like those shown in figure 2. Stitch and press the seam allowances toward the accent fabric.

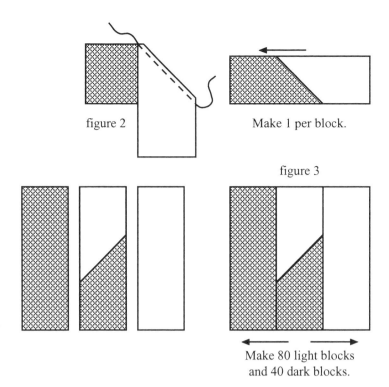

figure 2

Make 1 per block.

figure 3

Complete the blocks as shown in figure 3. Make eighty blocks with light background and forty blocks with dark background. Press the seam allowances away from the center section as shown by the arrows.

Make 80 light blocks and 40 dark blocks.

Arrange the blocks in twelve rows of ten blocks, rotating the blocks as necessary to make the pattern, and placing the blocks containing the dark background around the outside edges of the quilt to create a border effect. Sew the quilt together by piecing horizontal rows. Press the seam allowances in the directions shown below.

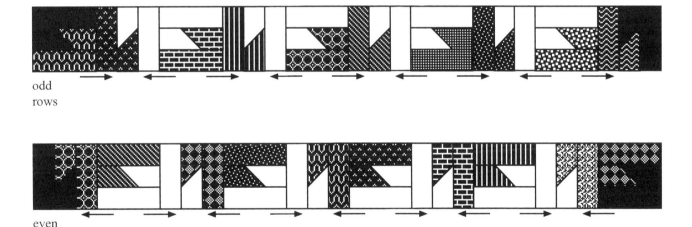

odd rows

even rows

Sew the rows together. Press the seam allowances to one side.

Options to Consider --

For a full/queen size quilt, make 224 blocks (168 with light background and 56 with dark background). Arrange the blocks in sixteen rows of fourteen blocks, rotating the blocks as necessary to make the pattern. For a more generous fit on a queen size, add a 4" to 6" wide border.

To make a quilt that looks like gift packages, make four blocks using the same two fabrics, and sew them into a larger 12" block.

Use a variety of dark large scale print fabrics to simulate wrapping paper and accent them with light small scale or tone on tone fabric "bows". Set the blocks squarely with sashing that is cut 2" wide and add a 5" wide border to complete the quilt shown below. Finished size of this variation is 54" x 68".

Friendship Braid

The size of the quilt shown on page 26 is 67" x 82".

Fabric Requirements

Cutting hundreds of trapezoids may sound like more work than you can imagine putting into a quilt, but read on. This is a very simple quilt. Once you have gathered the worms, cutting the trapezoids will take minutes!

56 worms - 28 light and 28 dark	
Sashing & borders	**2 1/4 yards**
Binding	**3/4 yard**
Backing	**5 yards**

Cutting -- Be sure you have read pages 10 through 13 before cutting!

Worms

Use the Omnigrid 96 triangle or template 4 to cut 4" (finished size) trapezoids and 4" (finished size) reverse trapezoids. See below for more specifics.

Cut four strips at a time. Because my variation of this pattern requires equal numbers of lights and darks, I choose to cut two light and two dark strips at a time. This way it is easy to cut more or fewer pieces to change the size of your quilt and you won't have to count!

Besides needing equal numbers of light and dark trapezoids, you need equal numbers of both values that are the reverses. To explain, look at the four pieces at the right. There is a light trapezoid (A), a light reverse trapezoid (B), a dark trapezoid (C), and a dark reverse trapezoid (D). After cutting the fifty-six worms there should be approximately 140 trapezoids of each unit.

To cut these quickly, neatly stack four strips that are folded in half, aligning the selvage edges and the long, cut edges on top of each other. You will be cutting through eight layers. The folded strips will yield an equal number of reverse units. See the general instructions on page 11 for more information on cutting the trapezoids.

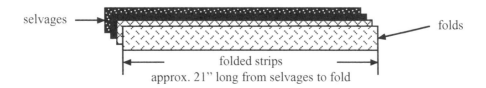

selvages →   ← folds

folded strips
approx. 21" long from selvages to fold

Piecing

Units B and C make the left half of the braid. Units A and D make the right half of the braid. Set aside the A's and D's while you construct the left halves of the five braids.

The braids will be constructed from the bottom to the top. Make all five at once so that you can chain piece.

Place a C piece, right sides together, on a B piece in the position shown in figure 1. Chain stitch five pairs like this. Clip them apart and *finger press* the seam allowances toward the light piece. Because of the bias edges, wait until the entire half of the braid is pieced to press with the iron.

The units should look like the one in figure 2 after the first seam. The arrow shows the pressing direction.

Since there is a light piece at the top of the braids, add a dark C piece to each. See figure 3. The two pieces will match at the top corner and intersect at the seam line at the bottom of the seam. Chain piece.

Clip the units apart. Finger press the seam allowances toward the piece you just added. The five braids now look like the one shown in figure 4.

Because the top pieces of the braids are dark, add a light B piece to each. Chain piece, clip the braids apart, and finger press the seam allowances toward the pieces you just added. The braids now look like figure 5.

Continue to add B and C pieces, alternately, until the halves of the braids are about six inches longer than your desired finished length.

Press the braid halves with an iron being careful not to distort the bias edges. Trim the dog ears.

Use the A and D pieces to make the five reverse braid halves. Start by piecing five units like the one shown in figure 6. These are started just like the other combination except that the dark and light pieces are in the opposite positions.

Add more A and D pieces to make these halves of the braids the same length as the B/C halves. Don't try to measure the braids. just count the number of pieces in each.

Press. Trim the dog ears.

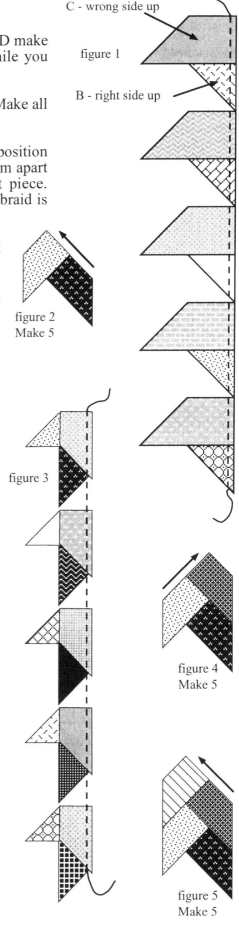

figure 1

C - wrong side up

B - right side up

figure 2
Make 5

figure 3

figure 4
Make 5

figure 5
Make 5

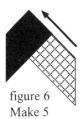

figure 6
Make 5

50

Trimming the braids as shown at the right staggers the seams so there are none to match. This is different than a traditional *Friendship Braid*, but it's a lot easier to construct. I first saw this in a braid quilt made by Brenda Henning. Read on for more specifics on how to trim the rows.

Notice how the corners of the pieces of the braid halves zig zag left and right of center. Trim the top of the braid halves 1/4" above a finished corner that is left of center, as shown by the line across the tops of the braid halves.

Trim all of the halves exactly the same way -- 1/4" above a corner that is left of center.

Trim the bottom of the braid halves 1/4" below the finished corner that is right of center, as shown by the line across the bottoms of the braid halves. Again, trim all of the halves exactly the same way.

When you place a B/C half and an A/D half side by side, they should be the same length, and the seam lines of the two halves should not meet each other. Sew the braid halves into pairs to make five braids.

Follow the instructions on page 30 or 31 for adding sashing and border strips. Use either option -- sashings and borders of equal widths or narrow sashings with wider borders.

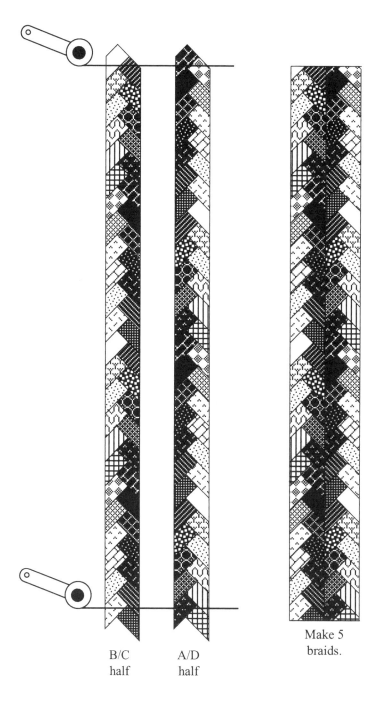

B/C half   A/D half

Make 5 braids.

Options to Consider --

For a full/queen size quilt, make seven braids instead of five. Make the braids about twelve trapezoids longer. This size will use approximately forty-eight light and forty-eight dark worms. For the sashing and borders, you will need two lengths, about five yards, of fabric. As always, these are ballpark figures. You may only want six braids and borders of your choosing.

Another option for making a full/queen is to complete the smaller quilt and then add a wide border as suggested for the *Cobblestones* quilt.

This is another great pieced border idea. The outer edge will need to be stay-stitched or have another border attached to control the bias edge. It will take a little designing to use this border, so I would recommend it only for experienced quilters.

Omit sashing and borders altogether and sew the braids directly to each other for a wonderful scrappy quilt like the one in the graphic on the next page.

The quilt shown below is approximately 51" x 64".

It will require about thirty-three light strips and thirty-three dark strips. Make six braids with twenty-seven each of the A, B, C, and D trapezoids. Sew the braids together without any sashing between them. Press the seam allowances to one side.

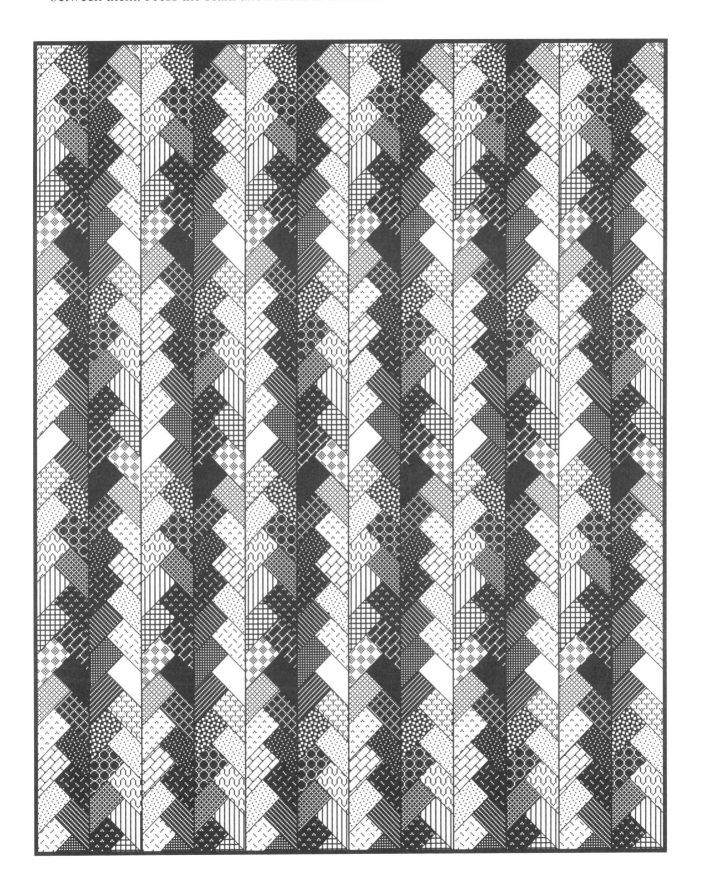

Sister's Choice

The size of the quilt shown on page 18 is 62" x 74".

Fabric Requirements

The inspiration for the stretch in the color scheme of this quilt came from a poem by Jenny Joseph, *When I am an Old Woman*. "It continues: I shall wear purple with a red hat which doesn't go...". It's a wonderful poem. Take time to find and read it.

The red fabric in this quilt is a bit off, but it makes you spend a little more time studying the quilt. I often recall a statement made in a workshop taught by Judi Warren in which she said that a successful quilt is one that makes you look at it for a time. The longer it holds the viewer's attention, for whatever reason, the more successful it is.

62 worms - 20 light and 42 dark

Sashing	1 1/2 yards
Cornerstones	two worms of the same fabric
Binding	3/4 yard
Backing	4 yards

Each block uses one light strip and one dark strip. The quilt shown on page 18 has twenty blocks in it. The other twenty-two strips of dark are are used for the piano keys border. Set the border strips aside to be used after the blocks are completed and sewn together with the sashing.

Cutting -- Be sure you have read pages 10 through 13 before cutting!

Light

From each of the twenty strips --

Cut eight 2 1/2" squares.

Cut eight 2" (finished size) half-square triangles, using the Omnigrid 96 or template 2.

Dark

From each of the twenty strips for the blocks --

Cut five 2 1/2" squares.

Cut four 2" (finished size) half-square triangles, using the Omnigrid 96 or template 2.

With the remainder of the dark strip *right side up and open to one layer* so that you don't cut any reverses, cut four 4" (finished size) trapezoids using the Omnigrid 96 or template 4. For more information on cutting trapezoids, see page 11 in the general instructions.

Cut 4 from each
dark fabric.
Cut no reverses!

Piecing

Gather all the pieces cut from one light strip and one dark strip and follow the instructions to piece a block. Trim the dog ears from the triangles and trapezoids before beginning to sew for perfect alignment and to save time. See page 13.

Sew a half-square triangle of light to each dark trapezoid. Press the seam allowances toward the trapezoid.

Make 4

Sew the four remaining half-square triangles of light to the half-square triangles of dark to make four half-square triangle units. Press the seam allowances toward the dark.

Make 4

Sew the half-square triangle units to a light square. Make sure the finished units look exactly like the one in the sketch when completed. Press the seam allowances toward the square.

Make 4

Sew the units you just completed to the triangle/trapezoid units from above to make the tulip-shaped sections shown directly at the right. Press the seam allowances in the direction shown by the arrow.

Make 4

Sew four pairs of light and dark squares. Press the seam allowances toward the light square.

Make 4

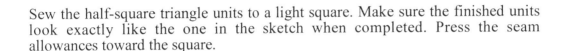

Arrange all the pieced units from above, and the remaining square of dark placed in the center, to make a Sister's Choice block. Piece the block by sewing horizontal rows. Press the seam allowances of the top and bottom rows toward the center section. Press the seam allowances of the middle row away from the center square.

Sew the rows together. Press the seam allowances toward the middle row. Repeat the above steps to make a total of twenty blocks.

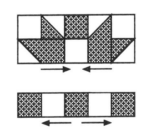

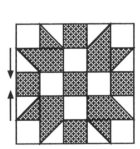

Make 1 from each of the twenty pairs of fabrics.

Measure your blocks to determine their average size. They should measure 10 1/2" at this time.

From your sashing fabric, cut forty-nine rectangles that are 2 1/2" x 10 1/2" (or whatever your blocks' average size is).

Cut the two 2 1/2" wide strips for the cornerstones into thirty 2 1/2" squares.

Arrange the sashes, cornerstones, and blocks to make the quilt four blocks wide and five rows long. See the picture on page 18. Sew the pieces into horizontal rows. Press the seam allowances toward the sashes in all rows.

Sew the rows together. Press the seam allowances toward the sashing rows.

Piano Keys Border

Sew the border strips into four panels, two with six strips and two with five strips. Press the seam allowances to one side.

Crosscut six 6 1/2" wide sections from each of the panels. Sew three sections of six rectangles and two sections of five rectangles end on end to make the top border of twenty-eight rectangles. Repeat to make the bottom border. Press the seam allowances to one side.

Sew the remaining sections into two borders, each with thirty-eight rectangles. Remove a group of four rectangles from one end of both borders to make the borders thirty-four rectangles long. Press the seam allowances to one side. Use these borders for the sides of the quilt.

Pin a side border to the left edge of the quilt top. It will extend 6 1/4" (three rectangles plus 1/4" seam allowance) below the bottom of the quilt. Sew the seam, matching the seam lines as necessary, but stop sewing about 12" before you reach the bottom of the quilt, leaving the end of the border free. Press the seam allowances toward the border.

Pin the top border to the quilt. Stitch and press the seam allowances toward the border.

Pin the second side border to the quilt. Stitch and press. Add the bottom border. Press.

Complete the partial seam that was made when you attached the first border. Press.

Options to Consider --

For a full/queen size quilt, make thirty blocks. For this variation you will need thirty light worms and seventy-two dark worms. The piano keys border will be made by piecing seven panels of six strips. Cut the panels for the piano keys border into four equal sections that are 10 1/2" wide to make a wider border. Use six sections each for the top and bottom borders and seven sections for each of the side borders. Purchase 1 3/4 yards for the sashing and 3/8 yard for the cornerstones.

The Sister's Choice block is very attractive when set on point. Try alternating it with plain blocks or pieced blocks that would compliment it such as a Framed Nine Patch like the one shown below. This block is simply pieced using 2 1/2" squares and 2 1/2" x 6 1/2" rectangles.

The sketch at the right shows a two fabric version which alternates the Sister's Choice and Framed Nine Patch blocks, as well as, using sashing and cornerstones. Are you up for the challenge?

Framed Nine
Patch block

55

What could be simpler than a whole quilt made of Framed Nine Patch blocks? The quilt shown below is made with twenty blocks. It measures 50" x 62". Place the lights and darks randomly for a fun scrappy quilt, or plan it as much as you like.

The blocks are sashed with forty-nine 2 1/2" x 10 1/2" rectangles and thirty 2 1/2" cornerstones, just like the *Sister's Choice* quilt. That means the same piano keys border would fit this quilt, too.

This is a great way to use up the segments that are left from the ends of used strips. Keep a box of strip ends, or better yet, cut them into squares and rectangles immediately, and save them until you have enough for a quilt made in the pioneer spirit.

56

Road to Oklahoma

The size of the quilt shown on page 20 is 64" x 80".

Fabric Requirements

Avoid overmatching the colors and values of the fabrics, and use a variety of scales for visual interest.

Dark blue	30 - 36 worms
Medium blue	10 worms
Yellow	10 worms
Light background	40 - 44 worms
Binding	3/4 yard
Backing	5 yards

Cutting -- Be sure you have read pages 10 through 13 before cutting!

I used only three fabrics in each Road to Oklahoma block: a dark blue, a light background, and either a medium blue or a yellow. The fabrics were placed randomly in the border blocks. You may choose to use your fabrics randomly throughout the quilt. The cutting instructions below are for fabric placement like the quilt shown on page 20.

Dark blue

For each of the forty-eight Road to Oklahoma blocks, cut two 2 1/2" squares and four 2" (finished size) half-square triangles. Use the Omnigrid 96 or template 2 to cut the triangles. For more information on cutting triangles, see page 10 in the general instructions. Cut one block from each of your worms and cut a second block from enough of the worms to make the forty-eight blocks.

Use the remainder of the dark blue worms to cut the following pieces for making the border blocks:
thirty-two 2 1/2" x 6 1/2" rectangles,
thirty-two 2 1/2" x 4 1/2" rectangles, and
thirty-two 2 1/2" squares.
Remember, these will be used randomly when piecing the border blocks. Cut each size from a variety of dark blues.

Medium blue

Cut the ten worms into .160 squares (2 1/2").

Yellow

Cut the ten worms into 160 squares (2 1/2").

Light background

For each of the forty-eight Road to Oklahoma blocks, cut two 2 1/2" squares, two 4" (finished size) trapezoids, and two 4" (finished size) reverse trapezoids. Use the Omnigrid 96 or template 4 to cut the trapezoids. For more information on cutting trapezoids and reverse trapezoids see page 11 in the general instructions. Cut one block from each of your worms and cut a second block from enough of the worms to make the forty-eight blocks.

Use the remainder of the light background worms to cut the following pieces for making the border blocks:
> thirty-two 2 1/2" x 6 1/2" rectangles,
> thirty-two 2 1/2" x 4 1/2" rectangles, and
> thirty-two 2 1/2" squares.
> Remember, these will be used randomly when piecing the border blocks. Cut each size from a variety of lights.

Piecing

Trim the dog ears from the triangles and trapezoids before beginning to sew for perfect alignment and to save time. See page 13.

Piecing one Road to Oklahoma block

This quilt is made with forty-eight Road to Oklahoma blocks. Twenty-four of them have a medium blue diagonal chain, and the other twenty-four have a yellow diagonal chain. Otherwise, all blocks are constructed in exactly the same way.

Select two 2 1/2" squares and four triangles of a dark blue; two 2 1/2" squares, two 4" trapezoids, and two 4" reverse trapezoids of a light background; and four 2 1/2" squares of either a medium blue or a yellow. These are the pieces necessary to make one block.

Sew a dark blue triangle to each trapezoid and each reverse trapezoid. Press the seam allowances toward the dark blue triangle. See figure 1.

Sew a square of dark blue and a square of medium blue (or yellow) to the appropriate ends of both "A" units. Press the seam allowances toward the squares. See figure 2.

Use the remaining 2 1/2" squares to make a four patch for the center of the block.

Sew the "B" units to two opposite sides of the four patch to make a section that looks *exactly* like the one shown in figure 3.

Sew the sections with the "A" units to the piece made in figure 3 to complete a Road to Oklahoma block. Press the seam allowances toward the middle row.

Repeat to make twenty-four blocks with medium blue chains and twenty-four blocks with yellow chains.

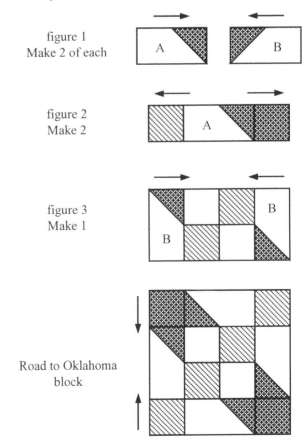

figure 1
Make 2 of each

figure 2
Make 2

figure 3
Make 1

Road to Oklahoma block

Piecing one border block

Each border block uses one 2 1/2" x 6 1/2" rectangle, one 2 1/2" x 4 1/2" rectangle, and one 2 1/2" square of dark blue; one 2 1/2" x 6 1/2" rectangle, one 2 1/2" x 4 1/2" rectangle, and one 2 1/2" square of light background; and four 2 1/2" squares of either medium blue or yellow. Use the fabrics randomly.

Arrange the pieces for a border block and sew into four vertical rows. See figure 4. Press the seam allowances toward the chain fabric (the medium blue or yellow), as shown by the arrows.

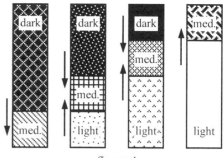

figure 4

Sew the rows together to complete the block. Press the seam allowances as shown by the arrows in figure 5.

Completing the top

Refer to the picture on page 20. Arrange the Road to Oklahoma blocks in the center of the quilt so that the top is six blocks wide and eight blocks long. Rotate the blocks as necessary to form the stars and chains. Notice the medium blue blocks and the yellow blocks alternate in a checkerboard fashion.

figure 5

Make 32 border blocks.

Sixteen blocks have yellow chains and sixteen blocks have medium blue chains.

Place the border blocks around the outer edges of the quilt to complete the pattern.

Piece the top by sewing the blocks into ten horizontal rows of eight blocks. Press the seam allowances of the odd rows to the left. Press the seam allowances of the even rows to the right. Sew the rows to each other and press the seam allowances to one side.

Options to Consider --

For a full/queen size quilt, make eighty Road to Oklahoma blocks and forty border blocks. For a more generous queen size, add a 4" to 6" wide border.

The border block is a great option to use by itself for a quilt. I call this block Up the Down Staircase. It is as versatile as a log cabin block when it comes to possible settings. Set it with or without sashing. See one of the possibilities at the top of the following page.

The Up the Down Staircase blocks work well as alternate setting squares for other blocks. Try using Sawtooth Stars (page 70), half with light background and half with dark background. Set them as shown in the graphic at the bottom of the next page.

The sashing in this quilt is cut 1 1/2" x 8 1/2" and the cornerstones are cut 1 1/2" square.

Alternate Up the Down Staircase blocks with stars made with light background and stars made with dark background.

Trees

The size of the quilt shown on page 24 is 60" x 80".

Fabric Requirements

The first time that I presented this pattern it was in the form of a mystery. It was taught in the fall. Clues for selecting the fabrics included the following: it is a seasonal scrappy quilt, and quilters may want to avoid using spring and summer florals, juvenile prints, etc. There were some wonderful quilts made during class. Two of them deserve note here. Suzy Hoffman made Christmas trees with a variety of holiday fabrics. And, Maribeth Richards educated us by showing that not only do black cats, ghosts, and flying witches spend time in trees, but candy corn and pumpkins grow in trees, too. Her use of Halloween fabrics for the trees delighted us all.

18 worms in tree fabrics	
Tree trunk fabric	1/4 yard
Background	3 1/2 yards
Border	2 3/8 yards
Binding	3/4 yard
Backing	5 yards

Cutting -- Be sure you have read pages 10 through 13 before cutting!

Worms

From each of the eighteen strips --

Cut three 2 1/2" squares.

Cut one 4" (finished size) trapezoid, one reverse 4" (finished size) trapezoid, two 6" (finished size) trapezoids, and two 6" (finished size) reverse trapezoids, using the Omnigrid 96 or templates 4 and 6.

Cut one 4" trapezoid and one 4" reverse trapezoid.

Cut two 6" trapezoids and two 6" reverse trapezoids.

Tree trunk fabric

Cut one strip 7" wide.
   Cut this strip into eighteen 1 1/2" x 7" rectangles.

Cutting

Background fabric

Cut three 18 1/4" squares.
> Cut these squares twice, diagonally, to make four quarter-square triangles from each.   Yield: 12 triangles

Cut two 9 3/8" squares.
> Cut these squares once, diagonally, to make half-square triangles for the corners of the quilt.   Yield: 4 triangles

Cut three 5" strips.
> Cut these strips into eighteen 5" squares.
>> Cut these squares once, diagonally, to make two half-square triangles from each.   Yield: 36 triangles

Cut nineteen 2 1/2" strips.
> You may need a few more strips if your fabric is narrow. Use these strips to cut the following pieces:
>
> eighteen 2 1/2" x 12 1/2" rectangles,
>
> eighteen 2 1/2" x 10 1/2" rectangles,
>
> eighteen 2 1/2" squares,
>
> eighteen 4" (finished size) trapezoids and eighteen reverse 4" (finished size) trapezoids, using the Omnigrid 96 or template 4.

Cut eighteen 4" trapezoids and eighteen 4" reverse trapezoids.

> seventy-two 2" (finished size) half-square triangles, using the Omnigrid 96 or template 2.

Piecing

Take the time to trim the dog ears from the small half-square triangles and all of the trapezoids prior to piecing. See page 13 for more instruction.

Pair the trapezoids of tree fabrics with the trapezoids and triangles of background fabric to make the units shown at the right. Make one of each for every tree block. Press the seam allowances toward the tree fabric.

Unit A — 4" trapezoid of tree fabric & 2" triangle of background

Unit B — 4" reverse trapezoid of tree fabric & 2" triangle of background

Unit C — 6" trapezoid of tree fabric & 2" triangle of background

Unit D — 6" reverse trapezoid of tree fabric & 2" triangle of background

Unit E — 6" trapezoid of tree fabric & 4" trapezoid of background

Unit F — 6" reverse trapezoid of tree fabric & 4" reverse trapezoid of background

Make 1 of each for every tree block.

Sew a 2 1/2" square of tree fabric to each Unit A, C, and E.* Press the seam allowances away from the squares.

*Use squares from a second tree fabric. Refer to the picture of the quilt on page 24 for suggestions on combining fabrics. I recommend that you keep the contrast low to avoid having these three squares look like a traffic signal in the center of your tree. If necessary, cut squares from other fabrics to accent the trees.

To make the tree trunks, sew the half-square triangles of background (those cut from the 5" squares) to both sides of the tree trunk rectangles. Press the seam allowances toward the tree trunk.

Make 18

Trim the trunk sections to a 4 1/2" square, centering the trunk along the diagonal. A small square with a diagonal line will help with this step. Use the template below for trimming, if you prefer.

Make 18

Construct the trees as you would an off-centered log cabin block, starting with the trunk. Add unit B to make the section you see at the right. Press the seam allowances in the direction shown by the arrow.

Make 1 for each tree.

Add the remaining sections in the following order, pressing the seam allowances toward each newly added piece: A + square to the top side, D to the right side, C + square to the top side, F to the right side, and E + square to the top side.

Finally, add the long rectangles of background fabric to the tree blocks and press the seam allowances toward the rectangles as they are added. Sew the 10 1/2" rectangles (G) to the top edge of the blocks and the 12 1/2" rectangles (H) to the right side.

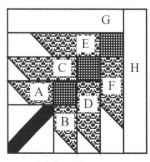

Make 18 trees.

To square off the trunk of each tree, place a 2 1/2" square of background fabric on the corner of each block, right sides together, as shown at the right.

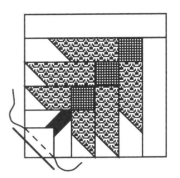

Stitch on the diagonal of the square as shown by the dotted line. Trim away the excess, leaving 1/4" for seam allowance, as shown by the solid line.

Press the seam allowances toward the small background piece.

Arrange the blocks on point with the large setting triangles. You will have two quarter-square side triangles left over. The half-square triangles are the corners of the quilt.

Sew the quilt together by making diagonal rows like those shown by the heavy diagonal lines. Press the seam allowances of the odd rows to the left and press the seam allowances of the even rows to the right.

Sew the rows together. Press the seam allowances to one side.

Add borders, as desired. The border on the quilt shown on page 24 is 7" wide. See page 14 for more instruction on borders with overlapped corners.

Options to Consider --

For a full/queen size quilt, make thirty-two blocks. That will require thirty-two worms, approximately twice as much background fabric, and 2 1/2 yards of border fabric. With the blocks set on point, as shown on the previous page, and the addition of a 10" wide border the quilt will measure 88" x 105".

Another setting option is shown below. This quilt uses twelve blocks. The 2 1/2" x 10 1/2" and 2 1/2" x 12 1/2" rectangles, as well as, the sew and flip step for flattening the bottom of the tree trunk are omitted. The setting triangles are cut half from background fabric and half from a dark fabric. The X triangles are quarter-square triangles cut from 15 3/8" squares, and the Y triangles are half-square triangles cut from 8" squares. This quilt of twelve blocks with a 6" wide border will measure 54 1/2" x 68 1/2".

This is a great block for holiday projects. Make the trees in fall colors to use for table runners or in Christmas fabrics for a tree skirt or decorative pillow. Use homespun plaids for Scotch Pines.

Four on Point

The size of the quilt shown on page 21 is 51" x 62".

Fabric Requirements

While in B J's Quilt Basket in Bend, Oregon, a large bundle of Thimbleberries fat quarters cried out for me to buy them. This is the quilt that resulted. To achieve the effect shown in the quilt on page 21, slightly more than half of the strips should be dark and the rest of them light, but use some medium value strips in place of a few of the light and dark strips for interest. Since I used fat quarters, I just cut two strips 2 1/2" x 21" to replace each worm.

44 - 48 worms

Border and setting triangles — 1 3/4 yards

Binding — 3/4 yard or scraps

> I used eleven 3 1/4" x 21" strips cut from various pieces in the bundle of fat quarters that I bought for this quilt.

Backing — 3 1/4 yards

Cutting -- Be sure you have read pages 10 through 13 before cutting!

Worms

From parts of all the strips, cut seventy-nine sets of four 4" (finished size) quarter-square triangles. Notice in the photo how the triangles are used in sets of four to create a Square Within a Square effect.

Use an Omnigrid 98, 98L or template A to cut them. *For more information on cutting triangles, see page 12 in the general instructions.*

From the remainder of all the strips, cut 126 pairs of 2 1/2" squares (252 squares, total).

You may choose to strip piece the four patches, but in order to allow for a scrappier and more random placement of the fabrics, I chose to cut the squares separately and chain piece the four patches.

Borders, side triangles, and corners

Remove the selvage from one edge of the fabric. Measure and cut four 4" wide strips, lengthwise, and reserve these for the borders.

From the remainder of the border and triangle fabric --
Cut eight 6 7/8" squares.
Cut these squares twice, diagonally, to make four quarter-square triangles from each. Yield: 32 triangles

Cut four 3 3/8" squares.

Piecing

Make sixty-three four patch blocks using two pairs of 2 1/2" squares for each block. Make the blocks with many combinations of fabrics.

Make 63

Use a design wall to lay out the triangles and four patches. See the sketch below. The quilt is assembled by sewing four patches and hourglass units in diagonal rows. This is much more accurate than piecing the individual Square Within a Square blocks. Once you have decided upon the fabric placement, piece the small quarter-square triangles into hourglass units and four corner units. See the top of the next page for instructions for making the corner units.

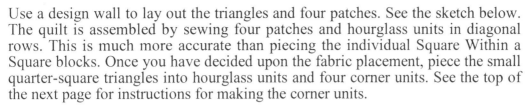
hourglass
unit

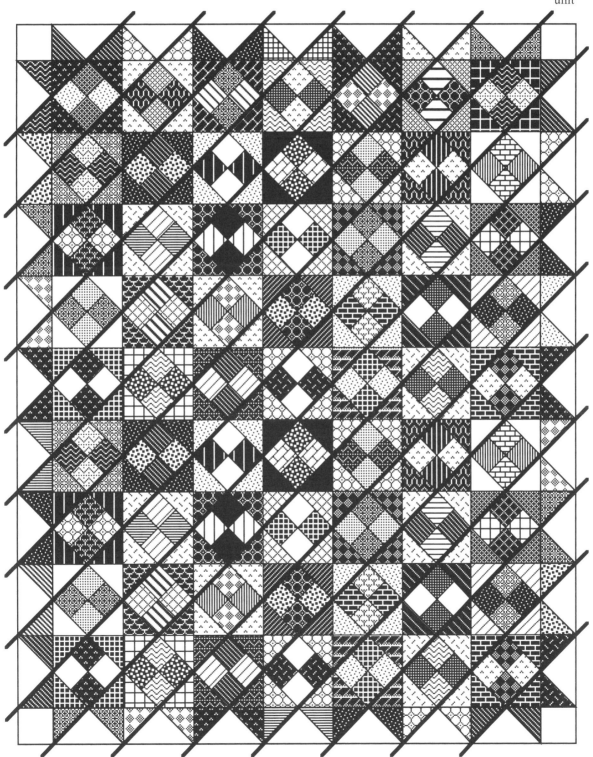

Follow the sketches below to piece the corner units. Press the seam allowances in the directions shown by the arrows.

Make 4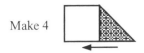

Make 4

Sew the units from the left into 4 sections.

Two of these units are for the upper right and lower left corners of the quilt.

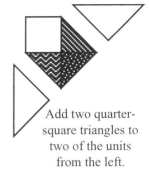 Add two quarter-square triangles to two of the units from the left.

Piece the diagonal rows shown by the heavy lines shown in the sketch on the previous page. Press the seam allowances away from the hourglass units in all rows.

Sew the rows together. Press the seam allowances to one side.

Add borders with overlapped corners. See page 14 for more instruction.

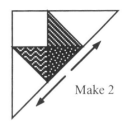 Make 2

These are the upper left and lower right corners of the quilt.

Options to Consider --

To make a queen size quilt in this manner with such small pieces would take a very long time, especially for the design wall work. Try using the units to make blocks that are a variation of an Ohio Star and set them with sashes or alternate plain squares. Depending upon your setting, a queen size quilt will require about twenty of these 12" blocks.

Cut the following pieces to make the Ohio Star block at the left. Use the Omnigrid 98 or template A to cut the quarter-square triangles.

Dark worm
Cut eight 4" (finished size) quarter-square triangles.

Medium dark worm
Cut six 2 1/2" squares.

Medium #1 worm
Cut six 2 1/2" squares.

Medium #2 worm
Cut four 4" (finished size) quarter-square triangles.

Light worm
Cut four 4" (finished size) quarter-square triangles and eight 2 1/2" squares.

Try other fabric placements in the Ohio Star block to see how many different looks you can achieve with the same block.

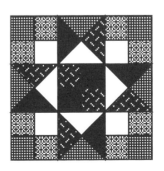

A simpler version of *Four on Point* is made by piecing individual blocks like the one shown at the right. Use four squares and four quarter-square triangles to piece each block. Press carefully to avoid stretching the bias on the outer edges. Using sashing stabilizes the bias edges and takes away the bulkiness that results when sewing the blocks directly to each other. Finished size of a forty-eight block quilt with sashes that are cut 2 1/2" x 6 1/8" and a border cut 3" wide is 53" x 68".

Star Sampler

The size of the quilt shown on page 17 is 47" x 56 1/2".

Fabric Requirements

All I can say about the fabric selection for this quilt is that it was begun on a quilting retreat at Diamond Lake, Oregon. It's funny what a little relaxation will do to you. While a minimum of thirty-five to forty worms are needed to make a quilt of twenty blocks, I used parts of many more for variety in my fabrics.

35 - 40 worms	
Border	1 1/2 yards
Binding	5/8 yard
Backing	3 yards

Cutting -- Be sure you have read pages 10 through 13 before cutting!

Organization is the key to this quilt. Here's my suggestion for the way to approach it:

This quilt is a good one for using a design wall. I suggest that you cut out at least six blocks and arrange them on the design wall before sewing any of them together. It is much easier to change your mind about the blocks before they are sewn.

Label four containers (shallow boxes or zip-closing plastic bags) with the letter of the pieces used in this quilt. Any piece that you cut and reject should go into its respective box or bag. Then, the next time you want to use that fabric, just retrieve the ready-cut pieces.

After you have designed six or more blocks, piece them and arrange the completed blocks on your design wall. Assess what you like about them and design more blocks. You will now be able to see if you need to add more of one color or fabric to achieve your desired results. Conversely, if you are using one color more often than you want to see it in the finished quilt, you can avoid putting it into the next round of blocks. Make four to six more blocks and reassess. Continue until you have made enough blocks to complete your quilt.

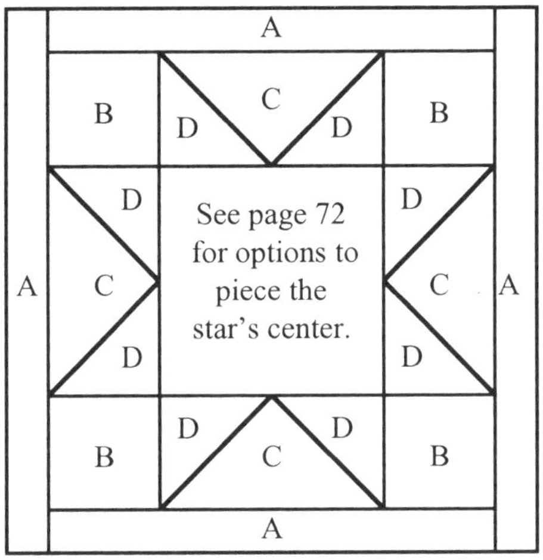

Piece	Cut size of piece
A	2 1/2" x 18 1/2"*
	* Cut one of piece #1 from each of twenty different worms and reserve them for framing the stars.
B	2 1/2" square
C	4" (finished size) quarter-square triangle, cut with the Omnigrid 98 or template A on page 75**
D	2" (finished size) half-square triangle, cut with the Omnigrid 96 or template 2 on page 75**

** See general instructions pages 10 through 13 for more information on cutting these.

Piecing

These instructions are for completing one 8" block. Consult the photograph on page 17 for suggestions on fabric placement. While I made each block using only one fabric for the background (the B's and C's), I chose to vary the star points, using one, two, or four different fabrics.

For each block you need the following:
> one pieced center (See the next page for options.),
> four B's and four C's for the background, and
> eight D's for the star points.
> *Use as many different fabrics as you'd like.*
> *Just keep them in their correct positions as you piece the star.*

Sew a D to each C as shown in figure 1. Press the seam allowances toward D.

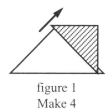

figure 1
Make 4

> *Hint:* Whenever possible line up the flattened end of the half-square triangle with the slightly flattened top of the quarter-square triangle (figure 2). One way to make sure that you can always do this is to trim the dog ears from all of the half-square triangles before piecing. See page 13. Then, they will align like those shown in figure 3. The dotted line shows the stitching line.

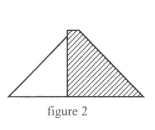

figure 2

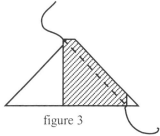

figure 3

Sew a second D to the units from above to make four flying geese units (figure 4). Press the seam allowances toward D. Trim the dog ears.

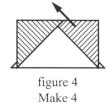

figure 4
Make 4

Arrange the flying geese units, the pieced center, and the four B's to make the star. Piece the star by sewing the units into three horizontal rows. Press the seam allowances of the top and bottom rows toward the squares. Press the seam allowances of the middle row toward the center unit.

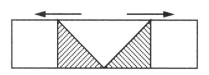

See page 72 for options to piece the star's center.

Sew the rows together and press the seam allowances away from the middle row.

Make 20 stars.

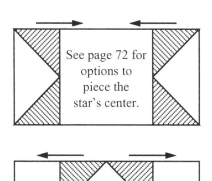

Options for the pieced centers of the stars

Four Patch

Cut four 2 1/2" squares. Use two or four fabrics.

Hourglass

Cut four 4" (finished size) quarter-square triangles (Omnigrid 98 or template A). Use two or four fabrics.

Pinwheel

Cut eight 2" (finished size) half-square triangles (Omnigrid 96 or template 2). Use two or more fabrics.

Broken Dishes

Cut eight 2" (finished size) half-square triangles (Omnigrid 96 or template 2). Use two or more fabrics.

Butterfly

Cut two 2 1/2" squares and four 2" (finished size) half-square triangles (Omnigrid 96 or template 2). Use two or more fabrics.

Check the next page to see how you can make even more stars by mixing and matching the pieced centers with the star point variations!

Star, stars, & more stars!

Use one, two, or four fabrics for the star points. By using a different center in each, see how many more blocks you can design.

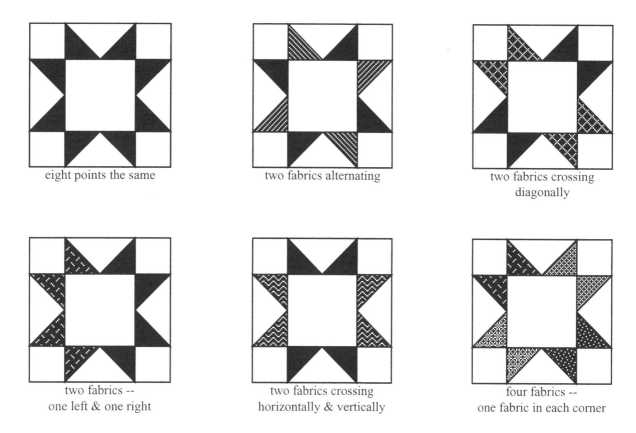

eight points the same

two fabrics alternating

two fabrics crossing diagonally

two fabrics --
one left & one right

two fabrics crossing
horizontally & vertically

four fabrics --
one fabric in each corner

See what happens when you fill in the centers! There are even more possibilities when you begin to make changes in the background pieces, too.

Finishing the Star Sampler

Cut the twenty reserved 2 1/2" x 18 1/2" pieces into two rectangles -- one 2 1/2" x 8 1/2" and one 2 1/2" x 10".
Cut these rectangles lengthwise into two 1 1/4" x 8 1/2" and two 1 1/4" x 10" rectangles.

Sew two shorter rectangles to two opposite sides of a star block. Press the seam allowances toward the rectangles. Attach the longer rectangles to the remaining two sides of the star. Press the seam allowances toward the rectangles. Repeat to frame all of the stars.

Arrange the blocks into five rows of four blocks. Rotate every other block a quarter turn so that there are *no seams to match* when the blocks are sewn into rows. Press the seam allowances in the directions shown by the arrows.

There are no seams to match when every
other block is rotated a quarter turn.

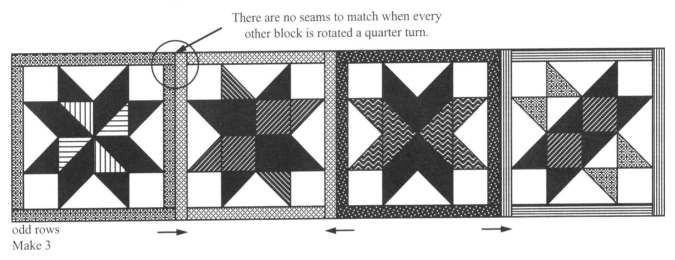

odd rows
Make 3

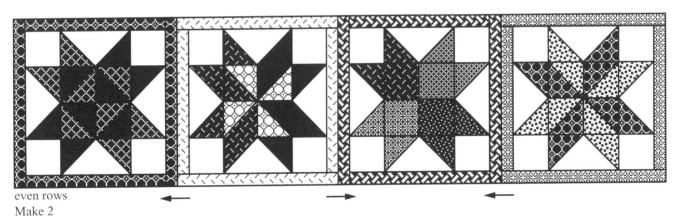

even rows
Make 2

Sew the rows together. Press the seam allowances to one side.

Cut four lengthwise panels 5" wide from the border fabric and add the borders to the quilt top. See page 14 for more information on adding borders with overlapped corners.

Option to Consider --

For a full/queen size quilt, you may want to use a different setting. Consider alternating the stars with plain blocks. Use a focus fabric or squares of many fabrics for a busier look, or float the stars by using more of a common background. Using this alternate block setting, a full/queen size quilt will require fifty stars and forty-nine plain blocks. Set the quilt nine blocks wide and eleven rows long. Add 8" wide borders and the finished quilt will measure 88" x 104".

Templates

Be sure to read page 5 in the introduction and pages 10 through 13 of the general instructions before using any of the patterns in this book. Use these templates for cutting triangles and trapezoids if you do not have the triangle tools.

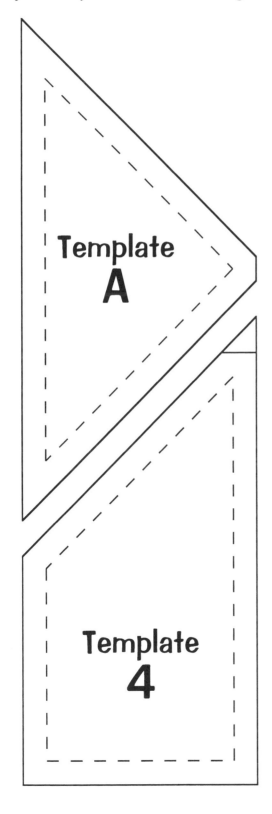

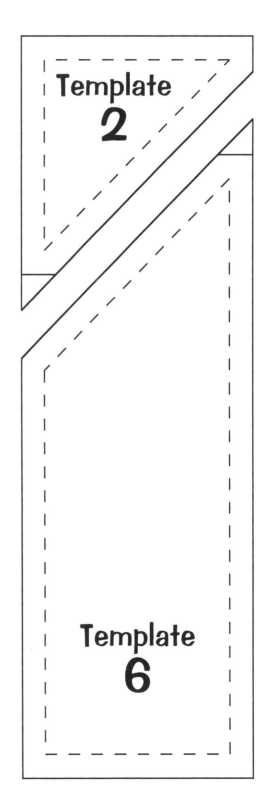

Debbie and daughter Erin take a minute to relax after photographing the cutting demonstrations. Erin cut the pieces and was the hand model while Debbie directed the shots.

About the Author

Debbie Caffrey is a self-published author of five books and eleven patterns. In addition, she has designed and published over seventy-five patterns in an ever-changing line of mysteries. Debbie has taught many energy-filled workshops nationwide for guilds and shops. These include Houston Quilt Festival, Minnesota Quilters' Conference, Festival of Classes in Bend, Oregon, and the Road to California. Debbie has contributed articles to *Traditional Quiltworks* magazine and has appeared on HGTV's television program, *Simply Quilts*.

Debbie and her husband Dan will return to the Middle Rio Grande Valley of New Mexico in the fall of 2000 where they will live near the small community of La Joya. They had lived in Anchorage, Alaska, since 1979 where they raised their children Monica, Erin, and Mark. Besides quilting, Debbie enjoys long walks and drives and experiencing new places. In New Mexico Debbie and Dan hope to spend many hours gardening and living an outdoor lifestyle.

Other books by Debbie Caffrey

Quilting Season
Scraps to You, Too
Blocks and Quilts Everywhere!
An Alaskan Sampler